THE LIFE-CHANGING MAGIC OF DECLUTTERING

A Practical Guide to Tidy Up Your Life and Clear the Clutter

Emma Grace Carter

Disclaimer

"Imagine if your home was a playlist. Would you rather have a carefully curated selection of songs you love or a random shuffle of music you don't even enjoy?"

"That is why decluttering without a strategy is like trying to climb Mount Everest wearing slippers, no matter how much motivation you have at first; it will all be lost before even reaching base camp."

"Think of your home as a garden. You don't just weed it once and expect it to stay perfect forever. It needs light tending, occasional pruning, and care throughout the seasons."

Table of Contents

INTRODUCTION

Welcome to The Life-Changing Magic of Decluttering. If you're holding this book, it's likely that you, like many others, are grappling with the clutter in your home—perhaps even in your life. But take a deep breath; you're not alone on this journey.

Seeing stuff lying everywhere is the most frustrating experience. I know this firsthand—piles of papers here, overflowing closets with clothes you haven't worn in years, and cluttered countertops filled with unused kitchen gadgets. It's chaotic, and it's tiring. You might wake up in the morning feeling like you are just spinning your wheels. No matter how much you clean things up, the mess keeps returning. It is an unending spiral that saps energy, robs you of a significant amount of free time, and often steals your peace of mind.

If any of this resonates with you right now, then this is where you need to be. I have written this book for you because I have experienced almost every condition you are in, and I am glad to offer you some good news. But before we forge ahead, let us all be brutally honest about the underlying issues we face.

Discovering the Problem: Why Clutter Gets Overwhelming

First things first: clutter is more than just an excess of stuff. Our emotional ties to those items often blind us. Understanding this can be a revelation. We don't hold onto clutter just because we like the items. It's the memories, the guilt from the money spent, or the fear of needing them one day. Recognizing these emotional barriers is the first step to overcoming them.

Here's the problem: regular or traditional organizing processes fail to solve the problem. You can buy all the storage bins you can find or invest in all the fancy organizing systems in the world, but all this does is relocate the clutter without addressing the real problem. The mess will return within a couple of weeks, leaving you feeling frustrated and defeated.

I completely understand where you are coming from. Deciding which items stay or go can be difficult because it involves much more than just stuff. You have emotions, memories, and history, and your self-worth is based on them. But, if you just try throwing stuff out without addressing these emotional barriers, it becomes more stressful, tiring, and impossible.

Here comes the good news: the clutter within your home does not have to be associated with the things I just mentioned. You can be free of those issues and from clutter.

Presenting the Solution: A Practical, Guilt-Free Approach

This book is a different one. I won't ask you to give up nearly all your stuff or impose extreme minimalism upon you. I won't guilt-trip you or force rigid rules on you. What I will do is show you a way to declutter without regret, creating a home that is peaceful, tidy, and organized.

I've developed a simple, step-by-step method that makes decluttering doable, no matter how busy you might be, how much you're in a hurry, or even if you have a significant attachment to your belongings. This system is simple, non-rigid, and practical. There are no complicated organizing systems to learn, no one-size-fits-all principles, and no severe expectations to live with as little as possible. This method has been tested by people like you—busy, overwhelmed individuals who thought they could never declutter but discovered they could.

This is not about becoming a minimalist but about retaining what is important and letting go of what bogs you down. I will guide you through the quick decision-making processes and show you how to maintain a clutter-free space for the long term. The best part of this proposition is that you will do it without guilt or being overwhelmed.

Why Trust Me?

You might wonder, *Who is this person trying to teach me about decluttering?* Well, let me tell you a bit about my story.

I started my journey as a teenager, cleaning houses to earn extra cash. It seemed like an easy job, but something interesting was underlying; clutter was more about emotion than the items. I watched many people wrestle with the desire to hold onto all sorts of stuff that occupied a room or two that they didn't use or even like. Their homes were beautiful, but the clutter stripped them of an elegant finish, making them seem stressful and chaotic.

Later, I moved to work in interior design, mainly thinking about redesigning rooms with stylish furniture and wonderful decor to transform them. But I soon learned that regardless of how much someone has spent on decorative objects and beautiful furniture, one of the most challenging exercises for me was to help my clients eradicate each bit of kitschy surplus they had in their lives. I witnessed them waver, feel guilty without realizing it, and cling to items they never intended to use. They remained stuck—not due to a desire to stay unkempt, but purely out of emotional attachment.

After all that, a time came when the lessons hit home so hard. As a mother of three who was practically drowning in toys, clothes, paperwork, and many other little things that came with a busy family, I found myself in a vicious cycle of cleaning and organizing, yet never making any headway. The clutter just kept coming back and wore me down.

That was when I realized I needed a system that wouldn't just organize but also reduce the mess. I wanted a house that felt comforting, functional, and easy enough to maintain, all through the occasional mess a family can bring. So, I piddled around, trying, learning, and simplifying. It has taken some time, but finally, I figured it out.

I found a way to organize the mess without imposing guilt once it was purged with a very practical, sustainable approach. I found a way to declutter without throwing everything out and without requiring being an ardent minimalist. I just embraced what I loved and released what didn't serve me—simple habits to keep clutter away.

It changed my life, and I am excited to share it with you.

The Benefits of Decluttering

Imagine waking up to a bedroom that invites peace and beauty with no mess. Picture yourself opening your closet to be warmly greeted by hanging clothes that fit your size, flatter you, and bring you great joy. Picture yourself cooking in a kitchen where everything you need is readily available from uncluttered cupboards.

Decluttering is more than just having a tidy home. It's about creating a space that supports your well-being, reduces stress, and makes everyday life easier. With less clutter, you'll experience:

- **Less Stress:** A clear space leads to a clear mind. Studies show that cluttered environments increase anxiety and mental fatigue.

- **More Free Time:** Less stuff means less cleaning and organizing. You'll spend less time searching for things and more time enjoying life.

- **Better Productivity:** A clutter-free space allows you to focus and be more efficient, whether it's at work, in the kitchen, or while tackling daily tasks.

- **A More Enjoyable Home:** Your home will become a sanctuary—a place that brings you comfort and peace instead of frustration and chaos.

You Can Do It!

The truth is that decluttering is never easy. It is hard work and demands resilience, patience, and a willingness to examine all attachments. But I promise you that this process is worth the effort and that you will never be alone.

I'm here to guide you through every stage to help you break free of all your feelings of guilt, fear, and overwhelm that prevent you from keeping your home serene. I will be helping you to take back your space, take back your time, and take back your peace of mind.

If you keep postponing, nothing will change. The clutter gets bigger, the stress mounts, and the endless cycle of cleaning to return to chaos starts all over. But it doesn't need to be that way.

You deserve a home that is calm, organized, and tensionless. You deserve to be released from the bindings of clutter. And you deserve the freedom that comes from letting go of what no longer serves you.

This book goes beyond decluttering and into a life makeover, one room at a time. So, take a deep breath, and let's get started. The journey to a clutter-free, peaceful, and organized home begins now.

CHAPTER 1
WHY DECLUTTERING FEELS SO HARD (AND HOW TO MAKE IT EASIER)

It may sound simple to declutter by just getting rid of unnecessary things. However, you would not be here hunting for a solution if it was that easy. You are stuck in this room full of stuff that no longer serves your purpose, unable to choose what to eliminate and feeling overwhelmed by the many things around you. Some possessions will always remain attached to you despite being a burden, whether guilt, fear, or nostalgia. The fact is that decluttering is not exactly about removing items from your life but dealing with their emotional attachments. This is what makes it difficult.

The good news? You're not alone, and you're not doomed to a life of clutter. This chapter will break down why decluttering feels so hard and how you can shift your mindset to make the process easier. By the end, you'll understand the hidden emotional barriers holding you back and have a practical way to move forward—without stress or regret.

The Real Reason Decluttering Feels Overwhelming

Most people think clutter is just about physical objects. But in reality, clutter is delayed decisions. Every item you hold onto represents a choice you haven't made yet, whether to keep it, toss it, donate it, or find a better place for it. When you have hundreds or even thousands of these tiny, unresolved decisions piled up around you, your brain feels overloaded.

Think of it like having 50 open tabs on your Internet browser. Your computer slows down, the system lags, and nothing runs smoothly. Clutter does the same thing to your mind. It creates constant background stress, making it hard to focus or relax.

We all have a story attached to each of our possessions, a reason why we acquired them in the first place. For instance, some items remind us of happier moments, whereas others remind us of failures, regrets, or lost opportunities. Thus, decluttering is like sorting out parts of yourself – it could be memories, identity markers, or even aspirations that haven't been fulfilled. This implies that you have held onto things that remind you of past times; still, you cannot throw them away unless you want to deny your past. That's why decluttering feels overwhelming. It's not just about cleaning up; it's about letting go.

Clutter represents more than just material possessions. It comprises memories, identity, security, and sometimes self-worth. That particular dress worn during a momentous occasion is more than just a piece of cloth—it carries reflections from that day. Also, when you hold a gadget that you never used, you feel an inner feeling of guilt about wasting money. How can you throw away something that was costly and never used? Why did you even buy it in the first place? The hardest part of letting go is not the stuff itself but what it stands for.

Storage solutions alone will not help in solving the problem. All the fancy bins, drawers, and organizers in the world can only help keep the items out of sight, but they do not deal with emotional attachments stored inside you. That's how the two differ: organized clutter and real decluttering.

Organized clutter occurs because you neatly put away stuff you don't need. Organized clutter also means you have stowed preferential items, i.e., family heirlooms, treasures from your youth, etc. The preferential items are things you no longer want out on display but aren't ready to dispose of. While giving an appearance of orderliness, this action does not deal with the underlying emotional load. True decluttering is all about letting go, not just keeping things orderly. It involves making peace with your past and providing room for the present.

Another reason decluttering appears overwhelming is mental overload. This means that your brain never stops processing all the visual information coming in from cluttered spaces; it's like a horror movie on repeat. This results in mental fatigue that interferes with making simple decisions, hence leading to choice paralysis—you can't figure out what to keep and what to discard. You're literally paralyzed with an overloaded processor under the sheer load of these decisions.

It is not because you are lazy or have no motivation. It is due instead to the emotional weight that comes with clutter. When you understand this, you will be more compassionate towards yourself and feel less pressure when decluttering. You are not just creating space but removing some heavy emotional baggage from yourself, which can bring a sense of relief and ease.

Emotional Barriers That Keep You Stuck

The hardest part about decluttering has nothing to do with what to keep or throw away but the feelings that keep you stuck. The biggest culprits are guilt, fear, sentimental attachment, perfectionism, and decision fatigue. Let's take a closer look at each one.

Guilt is a strong force that makes 'letting go' feel impossible. We feel guilty because we spent a fortune on the objects we never use. We feel guilty about gifts given to us by friends and family, even if they serve no purpose. We keep stuff around primarily out of sheer obligation, thinking that to be rid of them is slightly akin to disrespect or ungratefulness. But the fact is that the money is already spent, the gift is already given, and the purpose is to make you happy. There's no harm in letting it go when it fails to do that. You are honoring no one by keeping things out of guilt; you only create more mental stress for yourself.

During my research, I spoke to Lisa, a 42-year-old teacher who struggled to let go of expensive kitchen appliances she rarely used. She held onto them out of guilt, feeling that getting rid of them meant admitting to wasted money. But after finally donating them, she told me the guilt disappeared along with the clutter. Her kitchen felt lighter, and so did she. She no longer remembers the items she once agonized over, only the peace from letting them go and reclaiming her space.

Fear does not let you move forward and keeps you in the circle of «what if.» What if you need that old gadget one day? What if you regret throwing away the dress? The fear of needing something later leads to a «just in case» mentality where you hoard things, never to be worn or liked, all because of an overrated future scenario. There are salient questions you must ask yourself: how often have you really needed any of these «just-in-case» items? And if you did, would you remember where you stored it? More often than not, these items are forgotten once put away, and other solutions are found. Letting go does not mean losing security; it speeds up freedom from the unnecessary weight of «maybe,» bringing a sense of liberation.

One of the most difficult emotional barriers to overcome is **sentimental attachment.** This is why you keep pieces of porcelain that belonged to your grandmother even though they are not used anymore. It's the same kind of reasoning that makes you hold on to old love letters or even certain childhood toys without having any use for them now. Such stuff carries memories; getting rid of them would be like losing a part of your life. However, everything begins and ends within the mind! It does not mean that the past events are forgotten when we finally decide to let go of them. Letting go of these items does not mean forgetting the past but making space for the present and future.

Another hidden source is **perfectionism,** which puts you off-target for taking action. You either want to clear it all perfectly or do nothing about it. You tell yourself: "If I'm incapable of decluttering my entire room in one day, why should I start?" Thinking this way results in delaying everything until fear paralyzes you. However, you don't have to declutter perfectly! Decluttering is not an all-or-nothing kind of thing. Little steps matter; what counts is progress, not perfectionism. To overcome this, try setting small, achievable goals for decluttering and celebrate each step you take.

Shifting Your Mindset: Decluttering Without Regret

We're not decluttering from a position of loss; we are gaining freedom, clarity, and peace. Fear of regret is a major reason many people find decluttering arduous. *Could I need it someday? Will I miss it?* These are the kind of thoughts that keep you hanging on to things that don't serve you anymore. However, the secret to having no regrets is switching the mindset. Instead of asking, «Should I get rid of this?» you can ask, «Does this deserve space in my life?» These small shifts in perspective will make the biggest difference possible. This will shift your focus from losing to gaining.

Every item that survives takes up space and some energy and attention. If such items do not add value to your life, they cost you more than they are worth. Think of your home as a suitcase. If you overpack it with things you don't need, it becomes heavy and hard to carry. But if you only keep what's useful and meaningful, traveling through life becomes much more manageable.

When decluttering, focus on what to keep rather than what to lose. You shouldn't think you are giving up things you hold dear; it should be about cultivating an environment supportive of your present self. When you focus on keeping things that bring joy or serve a purpose in your life, the decluttering process stops feeling like a struggle or a sacrifice and instead promotes self-care.

Remember, losing objects does not have to mean losing memories. Memories live within you, not things. One way to retain the memory is to take pictures of sentimental items before giving them away. You honor the memory without carrying the physical burden.

Finally, embrace the idea that letting go is an act of gratitude. Thank those items for their service in your life, then let them go. The goal is to leave space for what really matters. With the right state of mind, you shift from seeing cluttering as punishment to seeing it as a form of self-comfort, allowing you to let go without fear or remorse.

The First Step to Breaking Free from Clutter

Starting is probably the hardest part. When you initially try to dig in and start sifting through the clutter, you realize the volume of useless stuff you must examine piece by piece. A paralyzing and staggering feeling sets in; it all seems so impossible. It's easy to quit right there and put it off for another time. However, remember, you do not have to do it all at once. The key to emancipation from clutter is starting small.

At first, choose the smallest, least emotionally attached area. It could be just a junk drawer, a bathroom cabinet, or even one shelf. Indeed, starting small ensures an initial start is made, generating momentum quickly. The momentum then goes on to ensure success with that small area. This success builds self-confidence and motivation to keep going. You don't have to declutter your entire home in one day. Just take the first step.

A powerful tool to help you get started is the **Two-Minute Rule**. The rule states that if a task takes less than two minutes, just do it now. This could apply to hanging something back up immediately, pulling expired things out of the cabinets, organizing a small stack of papers, etc. No matter how small the action is, it builds up over time and makes larger tasks seem more manageable.

In larger spaces, you can try the **Ten-Minute Decluttering Challenge.** Set a timer to run for ten minutes and concentrate on one tiny area. This helps prevent you from getting too anxious and adds some fun to the process. Once the timer goes off, you can stop or carry on, depending on how well you are doing in completing this task. This way, you take small and regular actions that result in significant changes over time.

Remember that progress is more important than perfection. You can take a breather or slow things down whenever you need it. The point is not to finish everything at once but to move forward in increments. If you start small and gain momentum, you will notice that the burden of cluttering lifts with every piece or area tackled.

CHAPTER 2

THE SIMPLE DECLUTTERING PLAN THAT ACTUALLY WORKS

As mentioned, decluttering is not about disposing of all you have or organizing them in perfect color-coded formulas. It is the act of arranging your space in such a way that it caters to you, not against you. But many people find decluttering difficult because they attempt to do everything at once or follow intricate systems that look impossible to uphold. Ultimately, they are left feeling worn out and discontented, and sometimes, the house appears messier than ever.

You are not alone if you feel this way. It's just that most methods do not work. Most decluttering methods fail due to their extreme nature, complex structures, or time consumption. But there is a better option.

This chapter will show you a simple, step-by-step system that makes decluttering practicable and effective, even for the busiest people. It is not about transforming your house into a minimalist showroom or spending all day sorting out each piece. It involves quick decisions, building momentum, and creating a light, functional, serene space. At the end of this chapter, you will have an established way of decluttering consistently.

Why Most Decluttering Methods Fail

I cannot overemphasize this: Most people fail at decluttering because they always try to do it all at once. This is what happens: They are ready to rock, so to speak, and within a few hours, they find themselves surrounded by heaps of stuff, feeling utterly burdened by fatigue. The mess ends up expanding, and they feel overwhelmed without the energy or time to continue. So, they throw in the towel, shove everything back into their closet and drawers, and feel defeated. It is not just discouraging; it is completely exhausting!

Trying to declutter everything at once leads to burnout. Making several decisions at the same time is mentally and physically exhausting. Decision fatigue sets in after some time, impairing your ability to think clearly or confidently because your mind can only take so much simultaneously. As a result, you start rethinking your every choice, hence feeling stuck and returning things 'just in case.'

The next most common reason people cannot achieve clutter-free spaces is their failure to recognize the difference between organizing and decluttering. Moving clutter from one place to another will not help when you just relocate it from point A to point B. This eventually leads to neatly arranged disarray, which may appear beautiful on the surface but is still tiresome deep down.

This has given rise to a widespread misunderstanding: *decluttering is not about getting rid of everything.* It is not about promptly pursuing minimalism or surviving with as few items as possible. The purpose of decluttering is to keep only what contributes real value to your life and to let go of the rest. It is about creating a home that supports rather than one that oppresses.

Imagine your house as a garden. Suppose you have too many weeds and twisted vines growing all over it. In that case, you can decide to cut or organize them. However, they will still be present, occupying some space and thus preventing flowers from getting enough air. Removing weeds brings about real transformation rather than simply arranging them neatly together. Similarly, decluttering means eliminating useless things instead of just reorganizing them.

A successful starting point for effective decluttering entails taking baby steps, gaining momentum, and using a method that makes decisions faster. Therefore, let's move right into it.

The Step-by-Step Decluttering System

Not to sound like a know-it-all, but the following steps have been tested and proven to work effectively as a system that can make decluttering a lot easier. I am setting the foundation for some of these steps and methods because they will be used throughout this book, especially when discussing how to declutter your home space. Don't worry if you find them in subsequent chapters; it's all an effort to ensure you understand the concepts perfectly before completing the book.

Step 1: Start Small and Build Momentum

As mentioned earlier, you need to start from the smallest area you can identify with less emotional attachment. It could be that study table or even the TV shelf. The main idea here is that you must start somewhere easy to ensure you can always make decisions without the burden of sentimentality or indecision. When you have completed this small area, celebrate it no matter how insignificant it might seem. Success builds confidence, and confidence builds momentum.

When I consciously wanted to start decluttering, I mistakenly tackled my entire closet in one go. Within an hour, I was surrounded by piles of clothes, feeling overwhelmed and exhausted. I gave up halfway through, shoving everything back in, and felt worse. That's when I realized I needed a different approach. So, I started small—one drawer at a time. It was manageable, and each tiny win motivated me to keep going.

Step 2: Use the "Keep, Donate, Trash" Method

Use the Keep, Donate, Trash technique once you've picked a small section to work on. This is simply a way of making decisions that eliminates guesswork and makes things faster. It works this way:

- **Keep:** Keep only what you love, use, or need often. If it doesn't serve a purpose or spark joy, it doesn't deserve space in your life.

- **Donate:** Give away things that are still in good condition but you don't need anymore. Other people can benefit from them, and donating allows you to eliminate them without feeling guilty.

- **Trash:** Discard anything that's broken, expired, or no longer of any use. It's time to throw it away if it's not worth donating.

Quick decision-making is essential to ensure that this method is effective. Don't overthink it. If you hesitate, ask yourself, "Would I buy this again today?" If the answer is no, then it's time to let it go.

Step 3: Follow the No-Mess Rule

Instead of feeling overwhelmed with trying to pull everything out at once to declutter, apply the "No-Mess Rule": Get rid of clutter in one small area per day without creating chaos in other parts of your house. This way, you can remain sane amidst chaos and avoid reaching a point where you feel like everything has turned into a big pile.

Step 4: Declutter First, Organize Later

Decluttering is different from organizing, so they need not be done separately. Declutter first so that the amount of your stuff reduces, then organize the rest. This saves time that would otherwise be spent organizing items that are no longer needed. It also helps you create a functional place that can be easily maintained.

The Golden Rules of Decluttering

When certain rules guide you, decluttering becomes easy and more efficient; these rules are there to simplify decision-making. The Golden Rules of Decluttering enable you to make quick and confident decisions rather than get stuck in emotional attachments or indecision. Here is how you can use them:

- *The 20/20 Rule:* Can you replace it with less than $20 and 20 minutes? Let that beast go, then. The rule is handy for eliminating things you keep when you "might need it one day." For instance, it can be your ten years of charging cords with your previous cellphone or that noodle maker you bought during the shopping marathon that you never use. It is inexpensive and can be purchased quickly if you need it later. This rule eliminates the fear of not having something later and lets you let go of whatever occupies space.

- *The 90/90 Rule:* Do you really need it when you do not use an item for 90 days and wouldn't use it over the next 90 days? Clothing, gadgets, and seasonal items are good examples. It forces you to be honest about what you actually use versus what you're holding onto "just in case." If a jacket has been living in some corner of your closet for the last six months, there's a strong likelihood that you won't be wearing it anytime soon. Letting go of something like that makes room for other items you own and use regularly.

- **The "Would I Buy It Again?" Test:** When unsure about an item, ask yourself, "Would I buy this again today at full price?" If not, dispose of it. This inquiry helps loosen the knot between emotion and an item's actual service or value. The test would compel you to consider the item's usefulness in your current lifestyle. If you would not exchange your hard-earned cash for it now, rest assured, it is a nuisance and is occupying usable space. This rule helps you curate a home with things that add value and joy.

- **The Five-Second Rule:** Act quickly without a doubt. If you wait more than five seconds, the object is not very important to you. Listen to your heart, let things flow, and never look back again. This rule makes decision-making easier and decluttering faster. It encourages you to listen to your instincts rather than overthink every choice. Keeping the process quick and intuitive prevents you from getting stuck in emotional indecision.

Following these guidelines will make your decisions more efficient, decrease resistance and fear, and simplify moving through the cleaning-up process. These rules give you a clear framework, helping you let go of unnecessary stuff and create a space that truly serves you. Also, note that these might be mentioned or reinforced in subsequent chapters. I am basically just spilling some of the tea for you to prepare yourself to understand them better, especially with specific spaces and items.

How to Make Decluttering a Habit, Not Just a One-Time Project

Decluttering is not something you do once but rather a way of living. This implies that you must develop habits to help you maintain a clutter-free home. It is possible to make decluttering a part of your life through these four powerful strategies:

- **Making Decluttering a Daily Routine:** Just spend five minutes daily returning items to where they belong. When you clear a countertop, sort out mail, or tidy up a small area within a few minutes, you have decluttered in a specific capacity. This prevents clutter from accumulating while also preventing it from becoming untidy. It's fast, simple and sustainable. When you make it a part of your daily schedule, everything remains in place without becoming overwhelming for you at any time. Consistency is important—doing something small over again eventually results in significant changes over time.

- **The "One In, One Out" Rule:** Always remove one old item whenever you add a new one to your home. This rule prevents cluttering by ensuring that before bringing anything in, you have to de cide whether or not it is necessary. Before you buy anything new, ask yourself what you will release to create space for it. Doing this stops you from making purchases based on impulse, thereby keeping your home balanced at all times. You will end up with fewer but better items because this rule teaches a sense of worthiness in quality rather than quantity. It ensures you don't have too many unnecessary things lying around. This approach allows you to enjoy life without being overwhelmed by material possessions.

- **The Decluttering Mindset Shift:** Decluttering must be framed in your mind as an act of self-love enough to become second nature. Instead of perceiving loss through decluttering, compare it with the gains on the other end: space, freedom, and a settled, peaceful mind. Decluttering isn't deprivation; it's about making a home that nurtures your lifestyle and well-being. When seen as a tool to simplify your life and reduce stress, it becomes a positive act of power instead of another dreaded chore. This simple shift in mindset will transform your relationship with stuff and allow you to release it without feeling guilt or fear.

- **Regular Maintenance Checks:** Schedule regular maintenance checks so the clutter doesn't pile up again. Once a month, spend 15-30 minutes doing a quick dash of decluttering. Blow through high-clutter areas like kitchen counters, junk drawers, or entrances. This helps prevent a build-up of mess and makes deep cleaning easier. It's just a sort of "refresh" for your home without the pressure of decluttering on a large scale. If you do it on a consistent schedule without letting the clutter build up, you won't suffer from being buried in so many things and instead will have an unwinding, serene, and organized space.

By developing these lifelong habit changes and mindset shifts, decluttering will become part of everyday life; it naturally helps you maintain a decluttered home with little effort. The more you practice these habits, the more it becomes second nature to give things up and live in a light and peaceful space.

CHAPTER 3

WHERE TO START (AND WHAT NOT TO DO)

We have all been there, at that point when you think, *"Today will be the day that I declutter!"* and then you find yourself at the center of your untidy living room, not knowing where to start. Those walk-in closets full of clothes, heaps of papers lying around here and there, and the kitchen countertop with no space left. You just give up. Netflix and chill suddenly sounds like a better alternative at that point.

That is why decluttering without a strategy is like trying to climb Mount Everest wearing slippers, no matter how much motivation you have at first; it will all be lost before even reaching base camp.

However, there is good news: you don't need to clean the whole house in just one day, nor do you need a perfect plan before starting. What you do need is a solid starting point—and to avoid some of the biggest mistakes that trip people up.

First, let me tell you what NOT to do so you do not set yourself up for failure early on.

Common Mistakes People Make When They Want To Declutter (Do's And Don't).

You may want to declutter so badly that you end up doing things in a complicated way. Here are four common blunders that people make while decluttering.

Beginning with Sentimental Stuff

This has always been a classic mistake for beginners. Most folks would think, *let me begin with my old love letters, childhood teddy bear collection, or even grandma's ancient plate set.* An hour later, they're sitting on the floor in tears, clutching an old teddy bear, reminiscing about the good old days. If you start with emotionally loaded items, you'll drain your energy before making progress.

Taking Everything Out at Once

We've all watched those home makeover television shows where the host empties everything from the closet onto the bed. It appears satisfying, but it actually creates disorder for most people. You go halfway, and then you get exhausted. You have other responsibilities, and suddenly, you will find yourself sleeping beside loads of clothes that are not folded.

Jumping From One Area to Another

This happens to the best of us because we are trying to be efficient: You go into the kitchen to declutter it, come across a pile of papers, pick them up, and walk to the office just to realize that the desk is full of clutter. Then you start arranging it only to find out that you have a heap of clothes that belong in the bedroom... and before you know it, you've begun five decluttering projects at once and finished none of them. It is a vicious cycle. You want to pick one area, stick with it, and don't move on until it's done. Momentum is your best friend here.

Waiting for the "Perfect" Time

Most people will tell themselves that for them to declutter properly, they have to free up an entire weekend or take the whole day off. Let's get real now: how often do you have a completely free day with nothing else going on? Waiting for the perfect time is *nothing* but a subtle excuse for procrastination.

The Best Places to Start Decluttering (For Quick Wins & Motivation)

The secret to starting without being overwhelmed is tackling the small «easy wins» first. Think of it like warming up before a workout—you wouldn't start with 200-pound deadlifts, right? Instead, one starts easy just to gain confidence and get going.

People often make mistakes by beginning with hidden storage places (such as garages or attics) where one cannot easily see the evidence of decluttering efforts for a while. However, decluttering gives the most satisfaction when you feel you are making immediate progress, so it's better if an individual starts with high-impact areas.

Starting With the Easiest Items (No Attachments Involved)

The goal is to make decluttering an easy process at its initial stage. You should begin with items you do not have any emotional attachment with –those that are just plain trash or unimportant. Some popular choices include:

- Expired groceries (storage unit, fridge, medicine chest)

- Old papers or magazines, out-of-date tickets, junk mail

- Broken or extraneous kitchenware

- Worn-out lingerie or worn socks

- Giveaways and freebies that you have never found useful (branded conference tote bags, hotel shampoo bottles, or pens)

One day, my sister-in-law and I were decluttering her kitchen together. She's a busy mom of three who constantly felt overwhelmed by the state of her home, especially with how chaotic the kitchen had become. We didn't attempt an entire overhaul; we just started with the infamous junk drawer. In about 10 minutes, we cleared out expired coupons, dead batteries, and mystery keys without locks. That tiny win boosted her so much that she couldn't wait to tackle the next drawer. She worked through the entire kitchen bit by bit, and it felt manageable for the first time in a long time.

High-Impact Areas (The Places You See Daily)

Re-organizing the spaces you use daily brings you an instant feeling of freedom. Rather than sort through an old basement storage box that has been untouched for years, concentrate on places like:

- Nightstands – Throw away old receipts, books you haven't completed, and chargers or electronics scattered all over.

- Kitchen countertops – Dispose of unnecessary kitchenware, out-of-order gadgets, or empty spice containers.

- Entryway desks – Take random keys off them, throw away junk mail that you never intend to open, and put away those shoes that are not supposed to be there.

- Car interiors – Dispose of used water bottles, dirty fast-food serviettes, toys, and anything else that doesn't belong.

When these frequently used spaces are clean, your home instantly feels lighter, giving you a sense of freedom and inspiration to continue decluttering.

Ten minutes Quick Declutter Plan

If you feel short on time, set a 10-minute timer and focus on one small area like a single bathroom drawer, your wallet (old receipts, expired cards), or one corner of your desk. All baby steps matter and help keep you going by fueling our impetus through quick accomplishments.

The Step-by-Step "Start Here" Plan

Now you know the starting point. I would like to recap and reinforce a few of the steps you can take to make your decluttering process less pressurizing.

Step 1: Choose a Small Manageable Space

Choose something little that can be completed at once, like a nightstand, one shelf, or your wallet. The aim is not to achieve perfection but to have immediate results.

Think of it like stretching before a workout—you ease into it before tackling larger tasks.

- Good choices: Junk drawer, spice rack, single bathroom shelf.

- Bad choices: Your entire attic, childhood memory box, or the basement.

Step 2: Apply the Keep, Donate, Trash Technique

As mentioned earlier, sort your things into three piles:

- KEEP – Items that you are currently using and like.

- DONATE/SELL – Items that are still in excellent condition, but you don't need them anymore.

- TRASH – Items that are broken, expired, or completely useless.

Step 3: Apply the "Would I Buy It Again?" Test

You already understand that this could be a simple but effective test for decision-making. Ask yourself: "Would I want to spend my money on this again if I didn't own it?"

Yes? Keep it.

No? Then let it go.

Doing this will keep you from feeling guilty about disposing of items you no longer need.

Step 4: Finish One Area Before Moving On

Don't make the mistake of running around different rooms. First, declutter one area; you can take a breather before moving to another place.

It is like finishing one episode in a series before jumping into another. It keeps you concentrated and helps you complete the task in the long run.

Step 5: Celebrate Small Wins

Decluttering is not only about removing things but is also related to making yourself feel peaceful at home. Ensure you reward yourself every time you make such baby steps by taking a coffee break, going for a short walk, or just staring at your newly tidied space. The goal is to make steady progress, not attain perfection.

Additionally, take before-and-after pictures, if possible, to motivate yourself further. You can post your progress on decluttering groups or share it with friends.

Overcoming the "What If I Need It Later?" Fear

One of the key obstacles to decluttering is dealing with the thought: What if I get rid of this and need it someday? This fear convinces us that every single item is a potential lifesaver, so we hold onto hundreds of unnecessary things—old manuals for electronics we no longer own, extra bedding "just in case," and expired spices we might use for a recipe we've never made.

Instead of thinking "I might need this one day," ask yourself:

- Is this item serving a real purpose in my life today?

- Have I used it in the past year?

- Would I even remember having it if I didn't see it right now?

Most of the time, the answer is no. If you're keeping an item for a hypothetical future scenario that may never happen, you're giving up space, peace of mind, and mental clarity in the present.

Let's break free from this "someday" mindset with logical and practical approaches, some of which have been discussed in the last chapter but buttressed here.

The 90/90 Rule

As earlier stated, pose these questions to yourself:

- Have I used this item in the last 90 days?

- Will I realistically need it in the next 90 days?

If the answer is 'no,' let it go.

For example, that blender you haven't touched in 8 months? You don't need it. That fancy dress you keep for events that never happen? Time to donate it.

I remember this stunning dress a special friend gave to me. It was a fully embroidered, royalty-standard dinner dress that took up about 30% of my hanging closet space. The emotional attachment towards the person who gave it to me and the elegance of the dress made me keep it for about 5 years, though I wore it just once. There was also the fact that I could not wear it to everyday events or activities. It would take a really special dinner party or date to wear it again, but I still held on to it. When I eventually donated this dress to charity as a decluttering attempt, it's funny how I didn't even miss or think about it for several months.

Create a "Maybe Box" as a Safety Net

I am reiterating this because I have tried it, and it works like magic. It's like giving yourself an exit strategy if you are stuck in the decision loop.

- Take all the items you're unsure about and put them in a sealed box.

- Label the box with today's date.

- Set a reminder for 30 days from now.

- If you haven't missed, needed, or even thought about those items, donate the box without opening it. That's how I got rid of the fancy dress.

Many people hesitate to declutter because they equate it with waste. But decluttering isn't about throwing everything in the trash—it's about keeping only what truly serves you. Think of decluttering as redistributing resources to people who will actually use them rather than hoarding them for a «maybe» that never comes.

Action Step: Find one item you've been holding onto "just in case" and apply these methods. You'll feel lighter instantly.

CHAPTER 4

THE BEDROOM – CREATING A CALM, CLUTTER-FREE SPACE

Walking into a luxury hotel room, have you ever felt instantly calm? The room seems like a sanctuary because of the well-arranged space, uncluttered surfaces, and crisp sheets.

Now, shift focus back to your bedroom; if you walk in there and start thinking: "Where should I place my legs?» because the floor is covered with clothes scattered all over or books (most unread), and piles of everything else – then something has to be done about it. Who says your room can't feel as soothing as that luxury hotel?

Your bedroom should never be the most stressful part of your home, but it often becomes one for many people. Rather than being a place solely for rest, it ends up being a dumping ground for unfolded laundry, unread books, and items that don't belong there. But don't worry, we're about to change that. Imagine the relief of stepping into an uncluttered sanctuary, free from the burden of unnecessary items.

This chapter will show you how to declutter your bedroom step by step to create an environment of peace, relaxation, and comfort that can help you unwind.

Why a Clutter-Free Bedroom Matters

What is the first thing your bedroom tells you in the morning when you wake up and the last thing at night before you sleep?

Is it telling you, *welcome to this peaceful place where you can rest, relax, and get rejuvenated?"?*

Instead, does it scream at you, saying, "Just look at the mess here! You'll be lucky to locate your socks this morning. Don't trip over the heap of unwashed clothes as you leave?"

Many people do not realize how much their environment impacts their mood, stress levels, or sleep quality. Your bedroom should be your haven, not a storage unit dump or anything else that does not belong there.

A Cluttered Room = Cluttered Mind

Studies have shown that excess clutter leads to increased stress and anxiety. Researchers at UCLA found that people living in messy environments had higher cortisol levels, the stress hormone. (UCLA Center on Everyday Lives)

And it makes sense—when you wake up in a chaotic space, your brain starts the day feeling overwhelmed before you've even had coffee. Just like a computer with too many open tabs, your brain struggles to process everything simultaneously. A clutter-free room is like hitting the reset button.

Clutter and How It Affects Your Sleep

A messy bedroom doesn't just cause stress; it can also disrupt your sleep.

- Excessive visual clutter equals overstimulation- The brain can't switch off as quickly as it should.

- Heaps of unfinished tasks, such as laundry or piles of half-read magazines, keep your mind restless.

- Unmade beddings mean discomfort- If your bed is buried under clothes and random items, you're less likely to get quality rest.

According to a study by the National Sleep Foundation, people who make their bed every morning have 19% greater chances of sleeping well than those who don't (National Sleep Foundation).

What's The Goal?

Just imagine walking into your bedroom and instantly feeling calm. No more messes or piles of unrelated items, just an orderly place to relax.

Here's our target:

- An uncomplicated, practical place meant for sleeping and resting.

- No missing socks in the morning, but a room that makes you feel harmonious and tranquil.

- Sleep soundly without any bothers running through your mind at night,

Your bedroom must be a safe sanctuary after a stressful day rather than adding to your stress.

Step-by-Step Guide to Decluttering Your Bedroom

Let's get down to business, a step-by-step process to convert your room into an attractive place. The main goal is to progress rather than attain perfection in this task. Remember, even a small change can bring about a significant difference. Consider this more of a renovation project rather than a marathon... You work on it gradually; before you know it, your bedroom will be like a haven for you. The process is simple and manageable, designed to bring you peace of mind.

Step 1: Begin With Clearing Off Surfaces

Before decluttering your closet or under the bed, address what you can see first: nightstand, chest of drawers, and any other surface where stuff tends to accumulate.

- Take everything off those surfaces and create a pile.

- Place back only what is important (a lamp, a book, or something dear to you).

- Use trays or small organizers to prevent clutter from creeping back.

You'd be surprised by the effect of this. I automatically feel a sense of calm when I wake up every morning to see my nightstand holding just the lamp and the one book I read before going dozing off. Even if I know I have a hectic day ahead, I feel more at peace upon waking.

Step 2: The Clothing Purge

Closets and dressers are often the most cluttered, and it might be time for you to cut down on clothes.

- If you have not worn it in a year, get rid of it.

- Does this look fabulous on me? If not, dump it.

- Be honest about "someday" outfits—hanging onto items that do not fit or suit your current lifestyle only wastes space.

Note that a cluttered closet doesn't mean you have more outfit choices—it just means you spend more time searching for what to wear.

Step 3: Decluttering Under the Bed & Hidden Storage

Out of sight should not mean out of mind. Under-bed storage is great, but it shouldn't be a dumping ground for things you forgot existed.

- Take everything out and sift through them one by one.

- Leave only seasonal or beneficial items in there.

- Do away with dust collectors—if you have not used one in

a year, you do not need it.

Step 4: Eliminate the Bedroom Clutter That Doesn't Belong

Your bedroom is dedicated to sleeping and relaxing, not to working or keeping gym equipment or as storage. So, if there are any such items, it's time to kick them out.

- Work papers, laptops, and unpaid bills >> Take them to a workspace.

- Kid's toys & any other random household item >>Take them back to their place.

- Exercise equipment that no one uses >> Donate or move it. Even if you use them, let them be in a more befitting location, like a guest room or garage.

Your bedroom should be a place where you can relax and calm down, not one that will keep reminding you of unfinished chores.

Step 5: Organization of What's Left

After clearing out most of the clutter, you want to use organizing systems to maintain that tidiness.

- Baskets or bins are good storage places for any unplaced items.

- Keep surfaces clean—fewer objects result in less clutter.

- Put away seasonal items separately from daily usage spaces to free up room.

Don't forget that decluttering is not about doing away with everything; instead, it is about retaining only what is useful for you and making your life more convenient.

Common Bedroom Clutter Traps (And How to Avoid Them)

After a thorough decluttering, certain habits can often cause the mess to return, just like a friend who overstays at your place and refuses to go. We must avoid this.

Thus, here are some typical bedroom clutter traps with advice on how to beat them.

1. The "Clothes Chair" Problem

This one, you know: it all starts from just one neatly folded jumper on the chair; later, it turns out that you've added a pair of jeans but never put them back into your closet so far. Then, the stack grows – piles of your clothes, which you intend to wear again before washing them. Before you know it, the poor chair is buried.

Solution? Get rid of the chair. (Kidding! ...Sort of.) Better solution? Hang, fold, or wash clothes immediately. You can also use a laundry basket for re-wearable items. One designated spot keeps them off the furniture.

2. Overfilled Closets & Drawers

This situation is easily recognizable, where your closet is literally filled to the brim. However, you still feel like you have nothing to wear. Decision fatigue comes as a result of too much choice.

Strategy: Stick with the one-year rule – if you haven't worn it, give it away. Organize your clothes according to the season and type to make them easier to find when needed. You can also use thin, identical hangers to save space and keep your clothes neat.

Imagine if your closet only held clothes that looked good on you, and you liked wearing them. Dressing would be a no-brainer every morning.

Chapter 7 addresses how you can effectively declutter and organize your closet.

3. Too Many Decorative Items

A pair of framed pictures is okay, but a dresser full of candles, souvenirs, trinkets, and dusty ornaments? So messy.

It's simple: only display those things that actually make you happy. Not because they just look good. Avoid putting up all decorations at once; rotate them based on seasons. Bedside tables should have only basic items such as lamps, books, or at most one plant. A clutter-free bedroom doesn't mean boring; it just means intentional.

Maintaining a Clutter-Free Bedroom

Well done! You have done the challenging task of decluttering your bedroom, making it a peaceful escape. Let's ensure it remains this way. Indeed, we all know how unruly disorder seems to crawl back in — albeit innocently — just a single sock out of place or a busy nightstand will suffice for you to find yourself in this maze again.

However, the beauty of having no clutter in your room is not in doing endless cleaning; instead, it involves just taking some basic actions occasionally.

- **The 5-Minute Nightly Reset:** If you have ever woken up disturbed by the state of your room, then a brief five-minute reset before sleep may be beneficial.

Here's how:

◊ Place clothes in the closet, laundry basket, or back on the hanger.

◊ Clean off nightstands and surfaces –return books; throw any trash away

◊ Check the floor real quick- anything out of place goes back where it belongs

This is basically "future-you" being kind to "morning-you." Waking up to a tidy room = starting the day in control.

• Making Your Bed Every Morning: It seems like it won't matter, but it's true. You want to do this for the following reasons:

◊ A made bed = instant tidiness

◊ It makes your whole room feel put together (even if there's still a mess in the closet)

◊ Studies show that bed-makers are more productive and sleep better. (National Sleep Foundation)

If you choose to keep your bedroom free of clutter daily, it becomes a habit that leads to faster results rather than just trying to declutter as a one-off occurrence. By making these habits second nature, your bedroom will stay a calm, peaceful space—without the effort of constant decluttering.

CHAPTER 5

THE KITCHEN & PANTRY – SIMPLIFY THE HEART OF YOUR HOME

Think of the time you need to make a delicious meal. You want a pan, but there are three lids on top of it, Tupperware containers everywhere without matching lids, and an air fryer that has never been touched since you bought it. It makes you mad when you find yourself in such situations.

Most people have the same issue with their kitchens; it's where most clutter accumulates unintentionally — extra mugs, duplicates of kitchenware, and misplaced pantry items that expired long ago. And yet, it's also the heart of the home, where we prepare food, connect with family, and start and end our days.

The point of this chapter is to show how to make the kitchen work for you instead of against you by bringing functionality back into it: you don't want any more searching for tools in your drawers; no more expired food or unnecessary items in overfilled cupboards.

Why Kitchen Clutter Is So Stressful

We don't often stop to think about it, but kitchen clutter isn't just an inconvenience; it's a daily source of stress. The silent frustration creeps in when you can't find what you need, waste time digging through overstuffed cabinets, or when cooking feels more like a chore than a joy.

Many of us accumulate way more than we use, filling drawers with mismatched utensils, keeping stacks of plastic containers with no lids, and letting pantry items sit untouched for years. The result? A space that works against us instead of for us.

- One thing that contributes to this is "decision fatigue." Every object in a disorganized kitchen requires your attention to decide where it should be kept, whether you should leave it for future use, or just generally make any sense out of the chaos. And this leads to unnecessary mental stress.

- "Wasted time": Have you ever spent way too long looking for the right pan, spice, or utensil? A cluttered kitchen eats up precious minutes every day.

- Wasted food, wasted money. It is not uncommon for people with stuffed cupboards to forget what they have, thus leading to food getting stale or spoilt and even multiple purchases of the same items.

Imagine entering a restaurant kitchen where no one seems to know where any item is placed. The head chef is looking for salt; the second chef goes hunting for a frying pan, while another cannot trace their cutting board. Would you even want to stay? That's precisely what happens when a home kitchen is filled with clutter—it slows you down, makes cooking feel stressful, and turns what should be an enjoyable process into a frustrating experience.

Not only does decluttering make your kitchen more attractive, but it also helps make cooking, cleaning up after oneself, and preparing meals easier. The goal?

- Space for cooking without stress and ease of access to all items.

- An organized pantry with only the essentials—no expired cans from way back.

- No clutter around, which saves you time and energy.

Step-by-Step Guide to Decluttering Your Kitchen

Let us create a functional, stress-free kitchen space. Efficiency is the key to dealing with kitchen mess; you should have a kitchen that works for you rather than a Pinterest-perfect one. This guide will take you through the exact steps of clearing your kitchen of clutter while avoiding feeling overwhelmed.

I laughed so hard when Stacy (an old friend whom I hadn't seen in a while) visited and, upon seeing my kitchen, couldn't help but exclaim, «How are you maintaining such a clean kitchen? I could never.» She was shocked to discover it was the simplest of things like these. These might sound basic, but trust me, following these steps will take you one big step toward serenity in your kitchen.

Step 1: Clear Countertops First

When you clear your countertops, your kitchen immediately feels and looks cleaner.

- Remove everything from your counters, then group similar items.

- Return only the basic things that you usually require when in the kitchen.

- Assign other non-counter items to appropriate places within your house.

Why? A clutter-free counter gives you more prep space and instantly makes your kitchen feel bigger, cleaner, and more organized.

Step 2: Purge Expired & Unused Food

How many expired or ignored foods are currently sitting within the walls of your kitchen pantry? For most people, the answer would be too many items.

- Begin with expiry dates–throw away anything no longer safe enough for consumption.

- Donate duplicates – do you really need five packets of pasta?

- Donate unopened non-perishables that you might not end up using.

Pantry messiness is tricky because it thrives behind closed doors. A quick purge saves money, reduces food waste, and simplifies meal planning.

Step 3: Unclutter Cabinets and Drawers

Random items usually get lost in kitchen cabinets. If you always search through piles of mismatched Tupperware lids, something needs to change. You want to try the following hacks:

- One Shelf at A Time Approach–Undertake small areas so you do not feel overwhelmed.

- Discard any extras–how many wooden spatulas or spoons do you ever use?

- Throw away anything that is either broken or not serving any purpose at all–It is time for them to go if they are chipped, cracked, or covered in dust.

Treat your kitchen like a toolbox; only have what you use often or consider essential because everything else makes it unnecessarily crowded.

Step 4: Organize What's Left

After you have cleared up the mess, the next thing on your agenda is to design a user-friendly kitchen. You want to put items that you use often within your reach. Daily dishes, pans, and utensils should be easily accessible. You want to employ simple storage systems. These include stackable containers, drawer dividers, and spice racks that make the place orderly but not complicated. Lastly, always label the items in your pantry to ease identification.

Time is money; hence, less time spent in a good kitchen setup helps cut costs and reduces worry. Your upcoming self will appreciate it!

Common Kitchen Clutter Traps (And How to Fix Them)

It's one thing to eliminate clutter from your kitchen space, but another is keeping it that way. Since the kitchen is a high-traffic space, it is almost impossible for clutter not to return unintended.

Below are some major kitchen clutter traps and how to avoid them.

1. The "I Might Need This One Day" Syndrome

We all have those gadgets or tools we bought because we thought they might come in handy one day but haven't used them in months. That fancy bread maker, the vegetable spiralizer, or the fondue set from your wedding registry (you know the one).

Solution: Simply put- if you have not used it over the last six months, you probably will never use it. Giveaway, sell, or gift out to someone who actually needs them. As previously noted, anytime you feel reluctant about giving something away, keep it in a box for 30 days- if it is untouched after this timeline, let it go; you do not need it. Your kitchen is your workstation. Useless tools just get in your way.

2. The Junk Drawer That's Taking Over

Junk drawers start small but quickly become a black hole of random batteries, takeout menus, rubber bands, and things you don't even remember owning.

Solution: Clean it out thoroughly. Categorize the entire lot as "Keep," "Trash," and "Relocate." You should use drawer dividers or little containers for everything to remain organized. Also, leave only important things in the drawer, like actual essentials, and get rid of the expired coupons and mystery keys forever.

It's okay to have a junk drawer. Still, if opening it comes with pulling out tangled spaghetti, you want to do something about it before it leads to further frustrations.

3. Too Many Dishes, Mugs, & Containers

How many coffee mugs do you actually use? And what about all those plastic containers without lids? These accumulate faster than you can realize.

Solution: Keep only what you regularly use. If your family has four members, what are you doing with 10 mugs?

Match lids with containers – otherwise, throw away unmatched items. Also, arrange your mugs and dishes neatly to be easily accessible to all family members.

Having fewer dishes helps simplify your life: less washing, less space for storage, and fewer cabinets dominated by clutter.

Maintaining an Organized Kitchen & Pantry

It can feel so good when you declutter your kitchen— until things start getting busy again. You buy more groceries and leave dishes everywhere else; your kitchen looks messy again. But as always, staying organized doesn't require a whole overhaul every few months. As I mentioned, controlling things just takes a few simple habits.

Think of your kitchen like a high-functioning restaurant—only what's necessary and frequently used stays in rotation.

The Weekly 5-Minute Reset

It was daily for your bedroom; now, you only have to do this weekly, and you'll see the difference in the clutter. The concept is basically the same.

- Set a timer for 5 minutes.

- Quickly sweep the countertops, drawers, and cupboards.

- Throw away expired food, dispose of any junk, and place every item in its correct place.

Developing this small habit ensures long-term organization. You do not want to procrastinate much because "I will do it later" mostly becomes "never."

Smart Shopping Habits: Buy What You'll Use

One of the greatest sources of clutter in the kitchen is getting much more than you will need.

- Before doing grocery shopping, make a list and strictly adhere to it. No more unplanned expenses that you might not end up needing.

- Rearrange items in the pantry in such a way that the

newest groceries are placed at the back so that the older ones will be the first to be used.

- Before purchasing, ask yourself, «Do I have space for this? Will I really use it, or is this an impulse buy?"

A clutter-free kitchen starts with mindful purchasing—because what doesn't come in doesn't need to be decluttered later.

CHAPTER 6

THE LIVING ROOM – HOW TO KEEP THE MOST USED SPACE UNDER CONTROL

Remember that moment you walked into the living room thinking you would just sink into your couch, but instead, you had to pick up the remote controls, shuffle a pile of mail, move unread magazines, step over a toy or two, or wade through a pile of dirty socks and shoes? That feeling can make your heart sink. Despite the idea that the living room is supposed to be a place of leisure and connection, we sadly often turn it into a junkyard that holds everything that lacks a place elsewhere or should have been returned to where it belongs.

Since it's a shared space, clutter accumulates here faster than anywhere else. This is where letters land, kids' items find a temporary home, and unfinished projects go to die, swallowed by décor that went from cozy to distracting.

This chapter will explore practical, step-by-step methods for removing clutter with smart organization and employing simple systems. These efforts will help maintain a welcoming and stress-free space, making your living room a place you're proud to show off to guests.

Why a Clutter-Free Living Room Matters

The living room is the life center of your home. It is in this room where you relax; it is in this room where you entertain guests and spend quality time with your family. But when it's filled with clutter, it creates more than just a messy space—it can actually affect your mood and energy levels.

- Clutter in spaces causes exhaustion of the mind; therefore, your brain wears out. In a disordered living room, your brain gets tired of processing each item you see, wasting your energy.

- More stuff = more stress. Studies have shown that cluttered environments increase cortisol (the stress hormone), making it harder to relax.

- A tidy space improves focus and enjoyment. Whether watching TV, reading a book, or lounging, a clutter-free space makes these moments more peaceful.

Your living room should feel like a breath of fresh air, not an endless to-do list.

As you already know, you don't have to become a minimalist to have a serene living room. The key is to create a functional, inviting living room that suits your way of life. This practical advice empowers you to take control of your living space.

- Each item should have its place, so you don't have to keep looking for your remote controls or chargers.

- It's easy to tidy up. Simple systems keep clutter from piling up.

- The space feels open and inviting. Less visual clutter = more calm.

Step-by-Step Guide to Decluttering the Living Room

The steps are almost the same as in other rooms. However, I'll still emphasize them for the uniqueness of the living room.

Step 1: Remove What Doesn't Belong

- Scan the room for items that belong elsewhere. Look for things that have drifted into the living room—shoes, laundry, kids' toys, office supplies—and put them back where they belong.

- Use the "Lost & Found" bin method. If your family members constantly leave their things in the living room, designate a basket where misplaced items go at the end of the day. They can retrieve their stuff, or it gets donated after a set time.

- Be ruthless and do away with items that have gone unused for the last several months. These might include old magazines, décor that are kept aside for special occasions, or even unused cables.

Your living room is the first place visitors see when they pop in at your house. Would you want them to see it as a peaceful retreat or a chaotic storage space?

Step 2: Clearing the Clutter from Shelves and Surfaces

- Let's begin with the coffee table. Remove any items on it that serve no purpose at all — such as stray papers, extra candles, or old coasters that are never used.

- Simplify bookshelves. Your bookshelves should showcase only your favorite reads, not a dumping ground for items. Keep those you adore; give away any that are gathering dust.

- Adhere to the law of "Less is more" regarding decor. Too many decorative touches can make a room look messy instead of cozy. Keep what you like most and eliminate things not aligned with your current aesthetic taste.

- You can also ultimately adopt the "Corrall It" Principle. The «Corrall It» Principle is about grouping items together to make your space look more organized and stylish. Instead of randomly placing things on shelves, you can use decorative trays to bring everything together neatly and elegantly. For example, you can arrange books, candles, perfumes, and small decorations on a tray to create a beautiful display. Adding a small vase or a special keepsake can make it even more charming, turning everyday items into a stylish and eye-catching setup.

Note that if you have to move anything just to rest your coffee cup, then it's time for decluttering!

Step 3: Taming the Hidden Clutter

- Drawers & cabinets: Go through one drawer at a time, throwing out any random remotes, old batteries, or anything else you have even forgotten you had.

- Storage baskets: Place similar items together — like all remote controls, cables, or books. These storage baskets ensure these things don't clutter up tabletops.

- Cables & chargers: Get cable organizers to avoid the tangled mess of chargers all over your living room.

As basic as these sound, I can attest to how they have helped put many things in order in my living room.

Step 4: Smart Storage Solutions That Work

- Buy multifunctional furniture. Consider coffee tables with storage, ottomans with hideaways, or TV stands with built-in shelving.

- Employ decorative containers & serving trays. Remote controls and magazines can stay in a simple basket on the coffee table without looking disorganized.

- Rotate seasonal decorations. If you love decorating, store seasonal pieces instead of displaying everything at once. It makes them more special when you bring them out.

Common Living Room Clutter Traps (And How to Fix Them)

Like any other room, the living room is a natural magnet to many sneaky, unsuspecting items. And more so because it's a general space that everyone uses and might be a bit harder to be strict about.

Here are three major culprits of clutter in your living room and their solutions.

Piles of Mail & Paperwork

This trap can start with a single envelope and build from there. Next, a magazine gets mixed in, and then, a receipt you want to keep for later that actually gets lost among the letters. Before long, you have a towering paper mountain on your coffee table.

- Create a simple mail system. For instance, have a single tray or container where all incoming mail gets placed instead of throwing it around randomly within your house.

- Deal with the mail immediately after you get it! This means throwing out junk mail, placing the bills in a folder, and important documents inside the "to do" envelope.

- Go digital where possible. Switch to paperless billing to eliminate unnecessary mail clutter. This particular one hits home with me, as incoming mail contributed significantly to the clutter I was coping with. I intentionally called almost all my billing companies and opted to receive paperless mail instead. I was pleasantly surprised at how much less clutter there was.

Toys Everywhere

If you have children, the living area can quickly become the place where their toys accumulate. This explosion of toys is another common trap that makes your comfy zone a disaster area.

- One way out is to create a toy zone. Don't spread toys around the whole room - instead, collect them in baskets or storage boxes and keep them in one area.

- You should have only a few toys in sight while others are stored away and rotated every few weeks. In fact, this way, kids will find things interesting while reducing clutter levels.

- You can also make things fun by playing the 'cleanup game' with the children. Set a timer for them and ask them to pick up toys before the timer goes off. You are decluttering while making it fun with your kids.

Decor Overload

Your favorite decor can make your place feel homey. Still, excessive amounts can make it chaotic, making it the perfect trap.

- You want to follow the «Less is more» rule. Choose a few meaningful decor pieces and let them be the 'room stars' instead of filling up every space on shelves or all over walls with different items. This can follow the "Corrall It" principle as described earlier.

- You should also adopt the "Swap & Store" system. Instead of displaying everything at once, store some decor away and rotate pieces seasonally.

Your decorations should enhance the overall look of your room, not compete with it.

Maintaining a Living Room Free of Clutter

As you already know, the easy part is decluttering, while the hard part is maintaining the serenity over time. You can't do without some of the pointers I gave in previous chapters for other spaces. Nevertheless, here are three infallible ways to prevent constant clutter reoccurrence.

The 5-Minute Daily Reset

To keep messes away, it is essential to do short daily resets.

- Set a five-minute timer. Choose your convenient time – after dinner, before bed, or just before visitors arrive.

- Put away anything that does not belong. Toss trash, fold up blankets left lying around, or anything else that found their way from other rooms.

- Involve the entire family. When everybody is on board with this, it takes even less time.

Involving my three kids in the cleaning process has definitely been an eye-opener, and it kind of takes away the pressure of intentionally trying to spend more time with them.

Setting Boundaries for Shared Spaces

One of the biggest problems with the living room is that everyone wants to go there, but no one wishes to clean.

- Be specific about expectations. Let your family know: "The living room is a shared space; we all need to keep it tidy."

- Have designated spots for everything, such as blankets or remotes and books, so there are fewer complications when tidying up.

- Gently enforce the rules. If kids leave toys out, remind them to return them to the toy bin. If your partner leaves socks on the couch (why is this a universal thing?), hand them over with a smile and a simple, "Nice try, but these don't live here."

Keeping your living room free from clutter requires cooperation among all household members. The more you make your family participate in the process, the better it will get.

Your living room must provide comfort, not a state of chaos. Through serious decluttering, addressing common clutter traps, and setting up simple daily habits, you have established the grounds for a space that keeps itself in order and exhibits a warm and inviting atmosphere. Above all, don't aim for perfection; aim for a progressive mindset. Things will get messy on some days, but it's okay. Mindfully follow the above practices; you will be in control more often.

So, please pour yourself a cup of tea, throw on a thick, warm blanket, light a candle or the fireplace, take that deep breath, and enjoy that living room, knowing it is as clutter-free as possible!

CHAPTER 7

CLOSETS & CLOTHING – STOP DROWNING IN «SOMEDAY» OUTFITS

We all know the struggle; your wardrobe is a battleground, and you're waging war daily against decision fatigue, lost socks, and clothes you've forgotten you even had. You go to pull out something to wear and, suddenly, you're faced with a torrent of "maybes": dresses you want to fit into again, outfits that you promised yourself you'd put on at some point but never did, things that materialized from nowhere and you have no idea how you acquired it.

Not only is the closet one of the most cluttered spaces in the home but it is also filled with things we accumulate because they are part of our identities.

Let's admit it: We only wear a small fraction of what we own. Studies show that most people rotate between the same 20% of their wardrobe, while the rest just takes up valuable space.

This chapter will help you simplify your closet and make each dressing moment effortless and without strain. You should end up freeing up your closet space from overfilling clothes and eliminating any guilt that comes with them – have only what you love and need in it instead.

Why Closet Clutter Is So Overwhelming

Ordinarily, clothes should not be difficult to put in order. They fold and can be hung or placed nicely in drawers. Nevertheless, it is common to find closets that are filled with clothes. But why is this so? Unlike other clutters, clothes are wrapped in emotions, self-image, and wishful thinking.

- The "Someday" Problem: "I'll wear this when I lose weight." "I might need this for a fancy event one day." We keep clothes that reflect who we were or want to be rather than who we are now.

- Decision Fatigue: You always stand in front of that closet for too long, trying to choose what to wear.

- Nostalgia Factor: Clothes are not mere fabrics but memory holders. It might be hard to let go of that dress you wore during your first date or even the sweater you wore back in college, even though you don't wear them anymore.

- The "But I Spent Money on It" Dilemma: You just want to hold on to that item because it cost you a fortune to purchase.

The secret/goal to decluttering your closet is to create a space that always fits your «current» lifestyle.

- Every item should be wearable, suit your style, and make you happy.

- You shouldn't have to search for what you need in less than a few seconds.

- Getting ready should not be complicated but rather enjoyable.

Step-by-Step Guide to Decluttering Your Closet

You know the drill, let's begin!

Step 1: Take Everything Out

This may sound slightly dramatic, but take my word for it; it is a vital step. The only way to truly see what you own is to take everything out of your closet and lay it on your bed, floor, or another surface.

- Why? Because if you keep stuff in drawers or on hangers, you can't conceptualize how much you actually own.

- Having all your clothes laid out before you makes it easier to make decisions while confronting the mess in your closet.

Step 2: Sort Items into Categories

Once everything is out, group them into clear categories to make the sorting process organized and efficient:

- Clothes: tops, trousers or skirts, various gowns, blazers, etc.

- Shoes like sneakers, heels, boots, or sandals.

- Accessories, including belts, scarves, and hats, should be together.

- Seasonal wear like winter coats, swimsuits, or holiday outfits.

Grouping makes things easier because you can quickly identify anything you have excessive and/or duplicates of.

Step 3: The Keep, Donate, and Toss Method

Our classic! At this point, you need to make decisions. Consider each item carefully before dividing them into three main piles:

- KEEP – Keep only those items that fit perfectly to your body shape while also enhancing your looks.

- DONATE/SELL – Clothes that are in good condition but never get worn (wrong size, wrong style, just not your vibe anymore).

- TOSS - Anything damaged, stained, stretched out, or beyond repair—you won't fix them, so let them go.

How to Make Tough Decisions

- Ask yourself: Do I feel good when I wear this? If you even hesitate for a second, toss it out.

- One-year rule: if it hasn't been worn for a year, why keep it?

- The "Would I Buy It Again?" Trick: If you wouldn't spend money on it today, why are you keeping it?

- Expensive but unworn: The money has already been spent, and you can't get it back. What's worse? You can't think of anywhere you will wear it anytime soon. So just donate it and free up space.

Step 4: Organizing What's Left

- Once you have gotten rid of everything unimportant, it is time to put back the rest so your wardrobe can be functional and easy to maintain.

- Frequently worn items should be placed at eye level to make them easily accessible.

- Use matching hangers to create a visually clean look (it really makes a difference!).

- Fold and stack items properly to avoid messy piles. You can fold clothes into compact, upright-standing rectangles to maximize space and visibility in drawers. The technique requires laying the item flat, smoothing out wrinkles, folding it into thirds or quarters, and shaping it into a neat, self-supporting bundle. This method saves space and makes it easy to see all stored clothes at a glance, reducing clutter and promoting organization.

- Storage bins can help you to store seasonal clothes without filling up your entire closet space.

Common Closet Clutter Traps (And How to Fix Them)

As always, you must recognize the major traps that make it hard to keep your closet decluttered. Here are three major closet clutter culprits and exactly how to fix them for good.

«Someday Clothes» – The Outfits for a Life You're Not Living

We all have them—those "someday" outfits we hold onto for when we finally lose weight, start going to fancy events, or change our personal style overnight. The only problem with this is that "someday" rarely comes, but the clutter stays.

- Solution: Keep clothes that fit your current lifestyle and body, not those you hope to use someday.

- Try the "Dress for Today" Challenge. Ask yourself, *Would I feel confident if I had to get dressed using only what's in my closet right now?* If not, it's time to let go of anything that doesn't serve you today.

- Box up your «someday» clothes. If you're struggling, store them out of sight for six months. If you don't reach for them, you don't need them.

Your closet should depict who you are now but not a past or future version of yourself.

Impulse Buys & Sale Items – The "But It Was on Sale" Excuse

Buying anything just because it looks good or is on sale is a trap we often succumb to.

- Before buying anything, consider whether you would have bought this at full price. If your answer is negative, you probably do not need it.

- Create a "24-Hour Rule" for shopping. If you find something you love, wait until the next day before purchasing it; chances are you will no longer be interested in buying it.

- Check your wardrobe before shopping; don't just purchase another identical black sweater like your five others.

Shoes & Accessories Overflow – The "More Is More" Trap

Shoes, purses, scarves, and belts are the underhanded culprits behind closet junk. We make ourselves believe that more alternatives = more excellent wardrobe choices, only to discover that we end up settling for just a few favorites.

- Solution: Set a realistic limit. If you wear only three pairs of shoes regularly, do you need twenty pairs? Just keep those you like and give away others.

- It is impossible to wear what you cannot see! Have hooks, trays, and maybe a simple pegboard to keep them visible and within reach.

If something is not being used, remove it because it occupies space unnecessarily. Discard everything except those few items you actually love and are used frequently.

Maintaining a Clutter-Free Closet

The real challenge will always be keeping all the decluttering you have done that way over time. How do you ensure this with your closet?

The 10-Item Rule – A Simple Way to Keep Your Closet in Check

- Pick 10 items each season and decide if you still need them or not. They can be old clothes, shoes, or even accessories unused for a while.

- Do I still wear this? Does it fit into my current lifestyle? If not, send it to charity or consider other uses for the item.

These will keep your closet updated and eliminate any chances of unnecessary clutter. Think of it like a regular "wardrobe check-up" to keep things in balance.

The «One In, One Out» System

This rule keeps your closet from overflowing again—and makes you think twice before impulse shopping. Buying new things is fun, but making space for them is essential.

Build a Wardrobe That Works for You – Quality Over Quantity

Rather than acquire an enormous collection of junk, invest in a select few that will be loved and used often.

- Shift your mindset from «more is better» to «better is better.» Do not buy ten cheap shirts; instead, opt for fewer, high-quality items that will stand the test of time.

- Stick to a color scheme or style that makes mixing and matching easy. This creates more outfit options with fewer pieces.

A wardrobe should be about practicality, not just accumulation. The less you have, the more intentional your choices become.

Your closet should be a place of ease, not stress. Every morning, getting dressed should feel effortless, not overwhelming. By decluttering, avoiding common closet traps, and adopting simple maintenance habits, you've set yourself up for a wardrobe that truly works for you, where every item has a purpose and makes you feel great. No more rifling through stacks of clothes you don't wear or feeling guilty about past shopping mistakes. You've created space, not just in your closet, but in your life.

Most importantly, decluttering isn't about having less but keeping what matters. Keep refining your wardrobe as your style and needs evolve, and don't let the clutter sneak back in. You've already done the hard part. Now, it's just about keeping it simple. So, enjoy your fresh, functional closet and embrace the ease of owning only what you love.

CHAPTER 8

SENTIMENTAL CLUTTER – LETTING GO WITHOUT REGRET

We all have that particular drawer, box, or entire room in our home that holds more than just stuff; it's a memory bank. It could be a stack of birthday cards, an old prom dress, or your grandmother's porcelain figurine collection that you've never displayed but can't bring yourself to get rid of. Sentimental clutter is the hardest to declutter because it feels like we're throwing away a piece of our past.

But let's be real: Are we actually cherishing these items, or are they just sitting in storage, collecting dust? If everything is special, then nothing truly is. Our loved ones wouldn't want us to be weighed down by guilt, keeping things out of obligation rather than joy.

This chapter expands on sentimental clutter, as mentioned in previous chapters. This will help you free yourself from the emotional weight of sentimental clutter while keeping what truly matters. We'll separate meaningful keepsakes from unnecessary baggage, find ways to honor the past without drowning in it, and create a home that reflects the life you're living now.

Why Sentimental Clutter Feels So Hard to Let Go

Well, first, find solace in the fact that you can deal with sentimental clutter. These objects are tied to people, places, and moments we don't want to forget. But let's break down why letting go is so difficult.

- Objects hold memories. A concert t-shirt reminds us of a great night, but eliminating it won't erase the experience. You should know that the objects are not the memories.

- Guilt keeps us stuck. Whether it's a gift we didn't like or something expensive we barely used, we feel obligated to keep it, even if it no longer serves us.

- Inherited clutter is especially tricky. It's hard to part with items from loved ones who have passed, but we don't have to keep everything to honor their memory.

- We fear regret. The "What if I need this later?" voice creeps in, making us doubt our decisions. But how often do we actually use or even think about these items?

The goal is to choose which pieces of your past deserve space in your present.

- You deserve a home filled with things that bring you joy, not guilt or obligation.

- You can honor loved ones without holding onto everything they owned.

- Your memories live in you, not in a box in the attic.

Step-by-Step Guide to Decluttering Sentimental Items

Let's go through a practical, step-by-step process to help you sort these items confidently. The goal here isn't to erase the past—it's to make space for what truly deserves a place in your life today.

Step 1: Gather Sentimental Clutter in One Place

Seeing everything at once gives you perspective. When sentimental items are scattered around your home, it's easy to convince yourself that each is special. But when they're all in one spot, you'll start to see patterns of what truly holds meaning.

- Set aside a few hours and gather all sentimental clutter into one space. This could include old photos, childhood keepsakes, inherited items, gifts, and anything else you're keeping solely for emotional reasons.

- Don't panic! You don't have to get rid of everything. This is just about gaining clarity.

Step 2: Identify What Truly Holds Meaning

Not everything that feels sentimental is worth keeping forever. Ask yourself these key questions to separate valuable keepsakes from emotional baggage:

- Would I miss this if I didn't have it, or do I just feel guilty getting rid of it?

- Does this item bring me joy, or do I feel obligated to keep it?

- Is it stored and forgotten, or do I see and use it?

- Would a photo of this item serve the same purpose as the item itself?

Step 3: Letting Go with Gratitude

Instead of thinking, "I'm throwing this away," shift your mindset to "I'm making space for what truly matters."

- The «Take a Picture» Rule: If an item holds sentimental value but serves no real purpose, take a photo before letting it go. This way, the memory stays, but the clutter doesn't.

- Repurpose sentimental items: Transform a loved one's old shirts into a quilt, or turn old greeting cards into framed wall art.

- Donate with intention: If you're letting go of a sentimental item, think about how it could bring joy to someone else. A donation made with love is better than keeping something out of guilt.

Your loved ones wouldn't want you to feel burdened by their belongings. Letting go of things doesn't mean letting go of love.

Step 4: Choosing the Best Way to Honor What You Keep

- Now that you've let go of the excess, it's time to honor the items that truly deserve a place in your life.

- Create a memory box for small sentimental items. Limit yourself to one box to avoid accumulating more clutter.

- Display meaningful pieces instead of hiding them in storage. If something is important enough to keep, it should be seen and appreciated.

- Digitize old photos, letters, and documents to preserve them without taking up physical space.

Common Sentimental Clutter Traps (And How to Overcome Them)

If you are not intentional enough, you'll find yourself stuck in a decision loop due to certain clutter traps attached to these sentimental items.

«But It Was a Gift!» – The Guilt of Letting Go

It's just an exercise in futility holding on to that sweater we'll never wear or that book we'll never read simply because of who gave it to us. The fear of appearing ungrateful keeps us stuck with things we don't even want.

- Remember that a gift has already served its purpose the moment it was given with love. You are not obligated to keep it forever.

- Reframe the guilt. Ask yourself: Would the giver want me to feel weighed down by this? Likely not!

- Find a better home for it. If you're struggling to let go, donate the item to someone who will use and appreciate it.

There was this recipe book a friend gave me after I had my last kid. It's supposed to help me prepare meals that will make me recuperate faster post-partum; I used the book for a few months and kept it in one of my drawers. During one of my decluttering exercises, it dawned on me that I would likely not have another child, so I had no reason to keep the book. Seeing my pregnant sister's excitement when I gifted her the book, I felt really good.

That is the point; there might always be another purpose for that sentimental item, but you just need to figure it out and let your space breathe better.

Inherited Clutter – Keeping Things Out of Duty, Not Joy

Losing a loved one is painful, and their belongings can feel like a physical connection to them. But keeping everything they owned isn't necessary to honor their memory.

- Choose a few meaningful items to cherish and release the rest. Keeping an entire wardrobe or furniture set won't bring them back. Still, a single cherished item can carry just as much sentiment.

- Find new ways to honor their memory. Repurpose old clothing into a quilt, turn jewelry into keepsake art, or create a shadow box with a few small sentimental items.

- Pass things along. If you have items that belonged to a loved one but don't personally need them, consider giving them to other family members who will appreciate them.

Your loved ones would want their things to bring you comfort, not stress.

Childhood Keepsakes & Old Love Letters

Your childhood stuffed animals, high school yearbooks, and old love letters can bring nostalgia and create unnecessary clutter.

- Ask yourself: Does this bring me joy today, or am I just keeping it because it reminds me of a time in my life?

- You don't need to keep every childhood trophy or school project. Choose a few special ones and let the rest go.

- Digitize where possible. Take photos of old letters, yearbooks, or artwork so you can preserve the memory without keeping the physical clutter.

Your past shaped you, but it doesn't have to take up space in your present.

Moving Forward Without Clutter Holding You Back

Now that you've tackled the sentimental clutter, it's time to ensure it doesn't pile up again. Here's how to move forward with freedom while keeping only what truly matters.

Decluttering as a Way to Make Space for New Memories

Our homes, just like our lives, are constantly evolving. By letting go of things that no longer serve you, you're making space for new experiences, new memories, and a home that reflects who you are today.

- Think of decluttering as an act of self-care. You're creating a space that brings you peace, not stress.

- Permit yourself to let go. You don't have to hold onto things just because you once loved them. It's okay to outgrow items, phases, and even sentimental objects.

The Freedom Mindset – Letting Go of Physical Items Without Losing the Emotional Connection

- Memories live in you, not in objects. Your best moments aren't tied to things; they're part of you and will stay with you whether you keep the physical reminders or not.

- Letting go doesn't mean forgetting.

- Think about what you'd want for your loved ones. Would you want your things to be a burden or a blessing if your things were passed down? Keep only what truly adds value.

How to Prevent Future Sentimental Clutter from Accumulating

Decluttering sentimental items once is an outstanding achievement, but how do you stop the cycle from repeating?

- Be mindful of what you bring into your home. Before keeping something for sentimental reasons, ask: Will this truly add value to my life, or will it become another item I struggle to let go of later?

- Create limits. Give yourself a designated space for sentimental items. It could be a memory box or a small section of your home. If it starts to overflow, it's time to reevaluate.

- Taking pictures will always be a great way to keep memories alive.

- Letting go of sentimental clutter is about choosing what truly deserves a place in your life. The memories tied to these objects live in you, not in the items themselves. By keeping only the things that bring you joy and meaning, you create a home that reflects the life you're living now rather than being weighed down by the past.

As you move forward, remember that decluttering sentimental items is an act of self-care. You are not erasing history; you are curating it. Be intentional with what you keep, honor your memories in ways that serve you, and, most importantly, permit yourself to let go.

CHAPTER 9

THE GARAGE, ATTIC & STORAGE AREAS – TACKLING THE «OUT OF SIGHT, OUT OF MIND» CLUTTER

Let's be honest: the garage, attic, and basement are where good intentions go to die. These spaces start with a purpose but, over time, become dumping grounds for everything we don't want to deal with. That treadmill you swore you'd use? The box of tangled Christmas lights? And let's not even start on the mystery boxes—you know, the ones you shoved into a corner years ago and never opened again.

We keep things because we might need them one day or because we don't have time to decide about them. But the reality is that most of these things aren't useful; they are just forgotten. Once clutter takes over these areas, they stop being functional. Instead of storage spaces, they become stress spaces.

Whether it's your garage, attic, basement, or storage closet, I will walk you through reclaiming these spaces step by step. You'll finally be able to find what you need, eliminate what you don't, and stop clutter from creeping back in.

Why Storage Spaces Become a Clutter Nightmare

Garages, attics, and basements started as organized spaces with clear intentions: somewhere to store holiday decorations, out-of-season clothes, tools, or keepsakes. But somewhere along the way, things took a turn. So how did we get here?

The «I'll Deal with It Later» Trap

This is the singular, most accurate catchphrase for clutter. When we do not know what to do with things, these spaces are convenient to keep them in the meantime.

- «I'll sort through this later.» Well, later never comes!

- «I might need this someday.» Do you mean, «I'll forget I even have it and buy a new one instead?»

- «This is too sentimental to throw away.» So why is it not important enough to display?

Storage areas should not be holding pens for indecision. Instead of delaying choices, commit to deciding what stays and what goes.

The «Just in Case» Mentality

We have talked about this. We hold onto things just in case we might need them in the future.

- If you haven't used it in years, you likely never will.

- Most things you keep "just in case" are inexpensive or replaceable.

- Keeping everything «just in case» means you can't find what you need.

Well, it's time to think of your storage space like a VIP club; only essential, useful items get in. Everything else? Time to let it go. Set a time limit for your «just in case» items. If you haven't needed it in two years, let it go.

The Accidental Junkyard Effect

Storage areas tend to attract random, unorganized clutter like old paint cans, half-broken tools, tangled extension cords, and furniture that's too good to throw out but not good enough to use. It becomes impossible to navigate the space, and you end up unable to find what you need when you actually need it. To avoid this, you want to declutter by category (tools, decorations, furniture, etc.) and remove anything that no longer serves a purpose.

Step-by-Step Guide to Decluttering Garages, Attics & Basements

Whether it's your garage, attic, or basement, the key to decluttering without losing your mind is breaking it down into simple, manageable steps.

Step 1: Identify the Essentials – What Actually Belongs in Storage?

Not everything deserves a prime spot in your storage areas. These spaces should be reserved for items that are truly useful and necessary, such as:

- Seasonal decorations – Holiday decor, winter gear, and seasonal sports equipment.

- Rarely used but necessary tools – Power tools or home repair equipment.

- Backup supplies – Extra light bulbs, batteries, and emergency kits.

- Sentimental keepsakes – A limited number of meaningful items.

- Properly stored outdoor gear – Camping equipment, bikes, and patio furniture.

What does NOT belong in storage?

- Random junk you're unsure about

- Boxes you never open

- Broken furniture, appliances, or electronics

Let it go if it doesn't serve a purpose, doesn't work, or hasn't been touched in years.

Step 2: The «One Box at a Time» Method – Avoiding Overwhelm

Decluttering an entire garage or basement in one day is a recipe for exhaustion. Instead, tackle one box, shelf, or section at a time.

- Pick one manageable area (a shelf, a single corner, or a stack of boxes).

- Sort items into four categories:

1. Keep items that truly belong in storage.Donate items in good condition so that others can use them.

2. Sell valuable but unnecessary items.

3. Trash anything broken, expired, or useless.

- Finish one section before moving on. Don't bounce from one area to another; it leads to burnout.

- Have a plan for donations and trash. Get things out of the house ASAP to avoid second-guessing.

Small, consistent steps will get you further than trying to declutter an entire storage space in one exhausting day.

Step 3: Handling Large & Bulky Items – What Stays and What Goes?

- Old furniture: If it's broken, beyond repair, or hasn't been used in years, it needs to go. Sell, donate, or trash it.

- Exercise equipment: Be honest; will you use that treadmill from 2009? If not, sell it or donate it.

- Appliances: If it doesn't work and hasn't been fixed by now, it's time to let go.

- Seasonal decorations: Store them in clear bins with labels so you know what's inside during the next holiday season.

Step 4: Organizing What's Left -Smart Storage Solutions

Once you've decluttered, it's time to set up a system that prevents future chaos.

- Use clear storage bins. You should be able to see what's inside without opening the lid.

- Label everything. No more mystery boxes! Use big, bold labels for easy identification.

- Invest in shelving. Floor space should be for oversized items, not random stacks of boxes.

- Store by category. Keep holiday decorations together, tools in one place, and sporting gear neatly arranged.

A little organization goes a long way in keeping your storage areas clutter-free.

Common Storage Clutter Traps (And How to Fix Them)

You will keep moving around in a clutter circle if you do not identify and tackle these common clutter traps that plague the storage areas in your home.

Boxes of "Unknown" Stuff

We have all shoved random items into a box, sealed it up, and promised to deal with it later. Fast-forward five years, and that box is still sitting in the same spot, completely untouched.

- If you haven't needed anything inside, do you really need to keep it?

- These mystery boxes take up tons of valuable space and make it impossible to find what you actually need.

Set a deadline for mystery boxes. They are useless if you don't go through them within a month. Open, sort, and deal with them now, not later.

Keeping Stuff for Other People

Raise your hand if you're storing your adult child's college furniture, your cousin's old treadmill, or your best friend's boxes of who-knows-what. I call it the "niceness trap." I remember when my house became an unpaid storage facility simply because I had a large detached house, and most of my friends and family didn't. Someone comes to spend a few days or weeks, and they leave something behind to keep for them.

These items occupy space in your home while their rightful owner completely forgets they exist. If someone really wants an item, they will find a place in their home. I am not saying you shouldn't be nice but set a firm deadline. If they don't pick it up, you donate it. No exceptions.

The «Just in Case» Stockpile

I sometimes find use for some items, even after abandoning them for a while. Still, these things are usually cheap items that an upgraded version may even be available, like extension cords, VHS Tapes, etc. Keeping them is just as much of a clutter trap as others.

- Most "just in case" items never actually get used.

- Keeping everything for a hypothetical future means you sacrifice present-day space and sanity.

- 95% of the time, you can replace it cheaply if you need something later.

This is where the 90/90 Rule comes in handy. Let it go if you haven't used it in 90 days and won't need it in the next 90 days.

Expired, Outdated, or Broken Items

Half-empty paint cans from 2003? A DVD player that hasn't worked in years? Bags of old clothes that never made it to Goodwill? These all scream trap!

Storage spaces become junk graveyards because we put off making decisions. If it's broken, fix it now or throw it away. If it's expired, discard it immediately. If you meant to donate something but never did, make that your priority today.

Maintaining a Functional Storage Space

If not handled systematically over time, the clutter will always find its way back in. Here's a simple system that prevents clutter from taking over again.

The Annual Decluttering Check-In

Decluttering once is great. But decluttering such storage spaces at least once a year is the secret to never having to do a full-scale purge again.

- Schedule an annual check-in. Pick a date—maybe every January or before the holidays—to quickly review your storage spaces.

- Set a timer for one hour. Go through shelves, boxes, and bins. If something is outdated, broken, or unnecessary, remove it.

- Don't let "someday" items accumulate. If you find things you meant to use but never did, let them go.

Treat your storage space like a garden—it needs regular upkeep to stay clean and functional.

Setting Limits – Stop Clutter Before It Starts

These storage spaces seem to magically fill up again because clutter will expand to fit the available space without limits.

- Create a rule: Set a clear boundary for how much stuff each category gets. Examples: One bin for sentimental items, not five or no more than two shelves for seasonal decor.

- Use visual cues: Label your bins and shelves so everything has a designated place.

- Be mindful of new additions: If something new goes into storage, something old should come out.

- When the bin is full, it's full. Setting limits keeps clutter from spiraling out of control.

Using Storage for What It's Meant For – No More Junk Dumps

A storage space should store things you actually use—not random clutter that's been banished from the main part of the house. If you don't use it, it doesn't belong in storage. Simple as that.

- Keep things accessible. Items stored too deep, too high, or too buried might as well not exist.

- Make organization easy. If putting something away takes too much effort, you won't do it.

Until I learned most of the points I shared in this chapter, my garage was a dumping ground for things I "wasn't sure about." I found it easier to deal with this stuff when I told myself, "If I wouldn't drive across town to pick it up, I don't need to keep it." That mindset shift helped me eliminate 70% of my unnecessary storage clutter.

Storage should be for useful, intentional items—not forgotten junk.

By decluttering with intention, setting limits, and checking in regularly, you ensure these spaces remain functional rather than overwhelming. Imagine opening your attic, garage, or basement and instantly finding what you need instead of wading through piles of who-knows-what. That's the power of maintaining a clutter-free storage space.

The key takeaway? If it's worth keeping, it's worth organizing. And if it's not, let it go. Your future self will thank you for staying ahead of the mess instead of letting it build up again. With a little regular maintenance and mindful storage habits, your home will feel lighter, your storage areas will stay functional, and you'll never have to do a massive cleanout again. You've got this!

CHAPTER 10
RULES & HABITS FOR A CLUTTER-FREE HOME

Decluttering your home feels amazing, doesn't it? It's like taking a deep breath after holding it for too long. You've sorted, donated, tossed, and celebrated those freshly cleared spaces. But as you already know, the real challenge isn't the decluttering but keeping it out.

This chapter is your gentle nudge toward building sustainable habits that make clutter feel unwelcome in your home. We're not talking about rigid systems or picture-perfect Pinterest routines, just simple, doable habits that quietly run in the background of your life. Think of them like brushing your teeth or making your coffee: small actions that make a huge difference over time. You've already done the hard part. Now, it's about protecting your progress and building a home that stays light, functional, and clutter-resistant for the long haul.

Why Clutter Keeps Coming Back

Decluttering is like dental hygiene. You can't just floss once and then declare your teeth healthy forever (although that would have been nice, wouldn't it?) The same goes for your home. Clutter doesn't magically stay gone unless you have a plan to keep it that way. And for most people, it quietly returns because of a few sneaky habits that don't seem like a big deal until the piles start growing again.

- **Impulse shopping.** That innocent "treat yourself" trip to your online shopping scrolls at 11 p.m. can result in ten new items you don't really need, but convince yourself you might. A mug with a quirky quote? A fourth throw blanket? "It was on sale!" has been the primary reason for acquiring multiple useless things that clutter up our home.

- **Invisible systems—or lack thereof.** If items don't have designated homes, they wander. Mail ends on the dining table, shoes pile up by the door, and random stuff clings to every surface like a determined houseguest. You want to develop automatic habits to put things where they belong before becoming problematic.

- **The power of small messes.** That one jacket on the chair? It turns into three. A stack of unread mail? Becomes a mountain. Before long, you're back where you started, wondering why everything feels so overwhelming again. This is where most people throw in the towel, not because they didn't try, but because they didn't build the habits that keep clutter at bay.

This is where the "One In, One Out" rule comes in. It's simply one of the easiest, most effective strategies to maintain order without overthinking it.

Quick Daily & Weekly Habits to Keep Your Home Organized

Instead of waiting until clutter gets out of control, you can integrate quick daily and weekly routines that take minutes but make a huge difference in maintaining order.

If you've ever walked into a spotless home and wondered how they do it, study, and ask questions, you'd likely discover they have consistent, simple habits that keep things under control before they spiral into chaos.

The 5-Minute Daily Reset

As a reminder, instead of letting the mess build up, commit to a 5-minute daily reset.

- *How it works:* Set a timer for five minutes and do a quick sweep of high-traffic areas. Put things back where they belong, clear surfaces, and tidy up anything out of place.

- *Why it works:* This short burst of tidying prevents clutter from snowballing. Plus, waking up to a neat space sets a positive tone for the day ahead.

The Sunday Basket Method – Keeping Paper Clutter Under Control

Paper is arguably one of the biggest sources of clutter. Mail, bills, receipts, school forms, and random notes seem to multiply overnight. Instead of letting paperwork pile up, use the Sunday Basket Method:

- *How it works:* Designate a bin or basket where you toss incoming mail, receipts, and paperwork throughout the week. Every Sunday, take 10 minutes to sort through it. File what's needed, pay bills, toss or shred anything unnecessary.

- *Why it works:* Instead of scattered paper clutter all over the house, everything is contained in one spot, and you deal with it once a week instead of daily.

The "Put It Back" Rule

Most clutter happens because things don't get put away immediately. Shoes get kicked off and left by the door. A jacket is draped over the chair instead of hung up. Books and coffee cups are left on the table. The easiest way to prevent this? The Put It Back Rule.

- *How it works:* If you take something out, return it as soon as you're done. This applies to clothes, kitchen tools, remote controls, and anything else that tends to get left behind.

- *Why it works:* It eliminates "later" syndrome—the habit of telling yourself you'll put something away later (which often turns into a growing pile of clutter).

The 10-Minute Weekly Declutter

A quick, weekly decluttering session stops clutter from creeping back in. This isn't a full-scale cleanout but a quick check to see if anything can be tossed, donated, or put back in its place.

- *How it works:* Pick one area each week, your junk drawer, bathroom counter, or a random shelf—and do a rapid decluttering session. Set a timer and remove anything that's out of place or unnecessary.

- *Why it works:* Regular check-ins prevent clutter from building up, so you never have to do another exhausting, all-day decluttering project again.

The key to a clutter-free home isn't perfection but consistency. These daily and weekly habits take just a few minutes but keep your space from becoming messy. If you stick with them, you'll find that maintaining an organized home becomes effortless, and you'll never feel overwhelmed by clutter again.

Smart Shopping Habits – How to Stop Bringing in More Stuff

Shopping is a big culprit of clutter. This is why you need to develop smart shopping habits for big purchases and everyday items like clothes, gadgets, and even kitchen tools.

- *Recognize impulse buying triggers.* We've all fallen for a "limited-time" sale or clicked "Add to Cart" because we were stressed, bored, or trying to feel better. Start noticing what prompts these purchases. Are you shopping because you need something or because you're avoiding something else?

- *Ask yourself this simple question:* "Would I buy this at full price, with cash, if no one else ever saw it?" If the answer is no, it's probably not something you genuinely want or need. Avoid buying something just because it's a "good deal." A cluttered closet full of $10 tops you never wear is still a waste.

- *Embrace a quality-over-quantity mindset.* Instead of buying five okay items, buy one great one. Not only will it last longer, but it'll also reduce the number of things you own and actually use.

- *Create a shopping pause rule.* Wait 24 to 48 hours before buying non-essential items. This delay helps break the habit of emotional spending and gives you time to reconsider whether it's worth it.

In short, the fewer unnecessary things you bring in, the less you have to declutter later. Thoughtful shopping is just as powerful as letting go, and it keeps your home clutter-free for good.

CHAPTER 11

WHEN YOUR PARTNER OR KIDS WON'T DECLUTTER

Decluttering would probably be a dream come true with fewer headaches if you lived alone in a Pinterest-perfect bubble. But in real life? Real life includes a partner who insists on keeping every random cable "just in case," kids who treat broken toys like sacred relics, and shared spaces that turn into mini landfills no matter how hard you try.

One of the most common frustrations I hear from readers is, "I'm trying so hard to declutter, but no one else in my house is on board." Working toward a clutter-free, peaceful home can feel incredibly discouraging when your loved ones seem to be working in the opposite direction. This chapter is about navigating that tension without guilt-tripping, nagging, or turning your home into a battlefield. Because yes, it is possible to get your family on board, even if they're currently clinging to their stuff like it's made of gold.

Why People Resist Decluttering

Before you launch a full-on intervention with your family, it helps to understand why they resist letting go in the first place. It's not just stubbornness (even if it feels that way on the tenth time you trip over your partner's mystery box of wires).

For many people, holding onto things feels like holding onto control. Your partner might keep things because "they might come in handy" or because tossing them feels like admitting waste. Your kids might resist parting with toys because they're emotionally attached or because giving them up feels like losing something they "might want later." Even though we've touched on this idea in earlier chapters, it's worth reminding ourselves:

not all clutter is just stuff; it's often tied to how someone sees themselves or what makes them feel secure.

There's also the issue of practicality. Some people are naturally more organized than others. Your idea of "just tidying up a bit" may feel overwhelming to someone who doesn't know where to begin. They might worry they'll throw away something important by accident or get judged for what they choose to keep. Others have lived through hard times, and keeping things represents safety and preparedness.

And here's a hard truth: forcing someone to declutter never works. It can spark resentment, push them to dig their heels in deeper, and damage your relationship. Instead of pushing them to change, the better approach is helping them feel safe enough to consider it, and we'll get to how in the next section.

Understanding the why behind the resistance helps you approach the situation with empathy instead of frustration. And that's the first step toward real, lasting change.

How to Lead by Example Without Nagging

Nagging never feels good for either party. You might think you're gently "encouraging" your spouse or kids to tidy up, but it probably sounds like a broken record playing at max volume to them. So, instead of trying to convince them with words, show them through your actions.

- Start with your stuff. Declutter your personal areas: the closet, your side of the bedroom, your workspace, without touching a single item that doesn't belong to you. Make your transformation noticeable. When your side of the room suddenly feels more peaceful, when you stop wasting time looking for your keys or stressing over piles, people take note. It's like silently planting the seed of curiosity.

- Next, claim clutter-free zones in shared spaces. For example, you might decide that the coffee table, entryway bench, or dining table will remain completely clear. These small, visible spaces become a visual contrast, almost like a breath of fresh air in a stuffy room. And without saying a word, you've created an open invitation for the rest of the family to follow suit.

- Instead of shaming or pressuring, casually share your wins. Say something like, "I cleared out my nightstand drawer today, and now I can find my charger!" or "Getting rid of that stack of magazines made the room feel bigger." These little comments said with enthusiasm, not sarcasm, can plant the idea that decluttering is a helpful, even satisfying, activity.

- You can also make a before/after photo collage and show them to your relatives unobtrusively in conversations.

You're not trying to be the household minimalist guru overnight. You're just quietly becoming a living example of the benefits. And trust me, when your calm becomes contagious, others will want some of it, too.

Encouraging Your Partner to Declutter (Without Arguments)

If you've ever tried to "help" your partner declutter, which turned into a full-blown standoff over a college hoodie from 2005, this section is for you. Here's the truth: trying to declutter your partner's things without their buy-in is like trying to rearrange someone's mind—it won't work and probably causes resentment.

So, instead of issuing ultimatums, let's talk about compromise.

- *Set boundaries, not battles.* For example, agree on a number of storage bins or drawer space for certain categories like T-shirts, gadgets, or tools. If it doesn't fit, it doesn't stay, but they get to choose what goes. This method avoids pressure while still limiting the clutter.

- *The "Just Box It Up" strategy.* If your partner doesn't commit to letting something go, suggest boxing it and putting it in the garage, closet, or a labeled bin with a date. If it's untouched for six months, it's likely not that important. This gives them time to detach without making an immediate decision under pressure.

- Also, remember the golden rule of peace: *Respect Their Space.* If your partner has a drawer full of old chargers or a shelf dedicated to collectible mugs, let it be as long as it's contained. It's okay if not every inch of your home resembles a Pinterest dream board. Decluttering is about shared comfort, not control.

Lead with empathy, not frustration. Your goal isn't to win an argument; it's to build a home you both enjoy. When your partner feels respected, not judged, they're far more likely to come around, maybe even without you asking.

Helping Kids Declutter Without Tears or Fights

Getting kids to declutter can feel like trying to convince a squirrel to give up its acorn stash. Every crumpled drawing, broken toy, and party favor somehow becomes "the most important thing ever." But it doesn't have to be a daily battle of wills.

- The key is to **make decluttering fun,** not a punishment. Turn it into a game: set a ten-minute timer and challenge your child to find five toys they no longer play with. For participating, offer a small reward: a sticker, a high-five, or a special bedtime story. Kids who feel involved rather than ordered around are more likely to cooperate.

- **Toy Rotation.** Instead of giving them access to every toy at once, store half in a bin and swap them out monthly. It keeps things fresh without the visual chaos. And it gives you a sneaky opportunity to declutter the toys they don't even miss when they're "away."

- This one's a game-changer: **teach them the joy of giving.** Talk about how another child might love the toy they've outgrown. Let them help pick out which toys to donate and even drop them off together if possible. It builds empathy and reinforces that stuff doesn't equal happiness.

Help them build the habit young, and they'll grow into adults who don't attach their self-worth to stuff. That's the real win.

Setting Family Rules to Prevent Future Clutter

If everyone else keeps bringing in more stuff, it's only a matter of time before the chaos creeps back. A few gentle but firm household habits can make a huge difference.

- Start with the golden standard: the «**One In, One Out» rule,** but make it a family affair. If your child wants a new toy, an old one gets donated. If your partner brings home another coffee mug, one has to leave the shelf. It keeps everyone mindful and helps cut down on impulse collecting.

- Next, focus on building a **clutter-free culture at home.** Talk openly about why you're choosing to simplify. Let the kids help with donation trips. Celebrate progress as a family by turning before-and-after room reveals into proud moments. When tidiness becomes a shared goal instead of just "Mom's thing," it sticks.

- **Setting limits is also key.** That doesn't mean being the Fun Police; it means having designated spaces. A toy bin that must close with the lid on. A shelf where only five picture frames can live. Boundaries give freedom because everyone knows what "enough" looks like.

- And finally, **rethink how your family approaches gift-giving.** Encourage relatives to give experiences instead of things: museum memberships, zoo passes, or even a sleepover coupon from grandma. Less wrapping paper, more memories.

Consistency, not perfection, is the goal. When practiced together, these small shifts can keep clutter from creeping back like an uninvited houseguest.

Decluttering with your family doesn't have to be a constant battle of wills. With the right mindset, gentle consistency, and creativity, you can turn your home into a place where everyone contributes to the calm, not the chaos. Remember, it's not about forcing change overnight. It's about creating small, lasting shifts in your household's thoughts about stuff and space.

Start with your own habits where you have the most influence. Show them what's possible, set the tone, and lead by example. Over time, your family will follow, even if at their own pace. And when they do? You'll have a clutter-free home and a team working together to keep it that way.

CHAPTER 12

DECLUTTERING AS A LIFESTYLE – MAKING SPACE FOR WHAT REALLY MATTERS

If you've made it this far, I want you to take a moment and genuinely celebrate yourself. Seriously, go ahead and do a little happy dance. You've come a long way from that first step of staring down a cluttered drawer, unsure of where or how to begin. But look at you now. You've cleared out rooms, built better habits, and started reclaiming your home and peace. However, this isn't the end; it's actually the beginning.

Decluttering isn't just something you do in a few weekends; it has to become a way of life. You're not just tidying up but choosing how you want to live. Every decision to keep less, buy less, and stress less is a quiet act of rebellion against overwhelm. This chapter shows you how to carry that mindset forward, not as a rigid routine, but as a lifestyle. For your convenience, this chapter summarizes all the life hacks we have discussed throughout your journey in this book.

The Real Benefit of Decluttering: More Than Just a Clean Home

Having a spotless home is great. But the true value of decluttering goes way deeper than aesthetics. It's not just about tidying up your space but clearing your life. When you reduce clutter, you reduce the amount of visual "noise" that constantly nags at your brain.

Think about it: every item lying around sends a message; «Put me away,» «Clean me,» «Use me.» Multiply that by a hundred random things, and you're exhausted before the day starts. Research has shown that clutter increases cortisol levels, especially in women, leading to more stress, fatigue, and less peace. A clear space really does help foster a clearer mind.

Decluttering also gives you back one of your most valuable resources: time. Less clutter means less time spent cleaning, organizing, and searching for things. That time can now be spent cooking a meal you love, playing with your kids, or just sitting with a cup of tea doing absolutely nothing—guilt-free.

But here's where it gets even better: your focus sharpens when your space is in order. You start noticing the things that matter more: relationships, goals, and even your own mental and physical health. Many people find that once they simplify their home, they also begin reassessing other parts of their lives. It's like decluttering permits you to stop surviving and start living intentionally.

I am not just saying these things to put words on paper or cajole you; I have lived this reality, so you can count on this being first-hand information. So yes, a clean home is lovely. But a life with more calm, focus, and freedom? That's the real magic of decluttering.

The Minimalist Mindset (Without Going to Extremes)

Minimalism often gets a bad rap: people picture cold, empty rooms with a single chair and a wardrobe consisting of three shirts. But real minimalism isn't about getting rid of everything; it's about keeping only what truly adds value to your life. It's about owning what you need, loving what you have, and removing the excess that creates stress and distraction.

Imagine if your home was a playlist. Would you rather have a carefully curated selection of songs you love or a random shuffle of music you don't even enjoy? That's what the minimalist mindset is about—being intentional with what takes up space in your home (and your life).

Intentional Living vs. Extreme Minimalism

You don't have to give away all your belongings or live with a single plate and fork. The goal isn't deprivation but being mindful of what you bring into your space. This means:

- Choosing quality over quantity means owning fewer but better things that serve you well.

- Letting go of the pressure to keep up with trends and constant consumerism.

- Creating a home that reflects your needs, not just storing things "just in case."

The real beauty of a minimalist mindset is that it shifts your focus from stuff to experiences. Studies show that people who spend on experiences (travel, hobbies, and personal growth) report higher happiness levels than those who constantly buy more things.

How Decluttering Transforms More Than Just Your Home

Many people don't expect it, but once they start letting go of the unnecessary, they begin seeing positive shifts in other areas of life.

Physical Decluttering Leads to Mental Clarity

Think about how you feel when you walk into a messy, overstuffed room. Now, compare that to the feeling of stepping into a well-organized, clutter-free space. Your environment influences your state of mind more than you realize.

- Research shows that clutter increases stress and anxiety by creating visual noise that overwhelms the brain.

- A tidy space allows your mind to relax, focus, and be more productive.

- People who declutter often feel more in control of their lives, making it easier to tackle other goals.

Re-evaluating Other Areas of Life

Something fascinating happens when you start decluttering: you begin questioning everything else in your life. As you sift through your belongings, you might catch yourself wondering:

- Why am I holding onto this job, relationship, or habit that no longer serves me?

- Do I actually enjoy how I'm spending my time, or am I just going through the motions?

- What would my life look like if I focused on what truly matters?

Many people find that once they declutter their homes, they start simplifying other aspects of life—commitments, relationships, finances, and even how they spend their time.

The Freedom of Having Less

I have said this many times: decluttering is about gaining more freedom.

- With fewer belongings, you spend less time cleaning, organizing, and searching for lost things.

- A clutter-free space makes it easier to appreciate what you already have, reducing the need to buy more constantly.

- You gain more time, energy, and mental space to focus on experiences, passions, and people who truly matter.

At its core, decluttering isn't just about making room in your home but making room for a more fulfilling, intentional life.

If you've made it this far, I want to say something loud and clear: I'm so proud of you. You consciously chose to take back control of your space, your peace, and your priorities. And that's no small thing.

Decluttering is a mindset, a shift in how you relate to your stuff and your space. There will be days when you feel super motivated and want to tackle an entire closet. And there will be days when you can only manage putting away your shoes or clearing off one corner of a countertop. Both are valid. Both count. Progress is still progress, no matter how small.

Remember: this journey isn't about perfection but intention. It's not about having the cleanest house on the block but creating a home that makes you feel calm, supported, and empowered. It's about making room for joy, space for creativity, and time for what truly matters. That's the heart of this entire book.

So take a deep breath, look around your home, and feel proud. You've done something powerful. You've chosen clarity over chaos. From here on out, you're not just tidying; you're thriving.

Let this be your new beginning. You've got this.

CONCLUSION
YOUR NEW CLUTTER-FREE LIFE BEGINS NOW

You made it to the end. That alone is something worth celebrating. You've taken the time, the energy, and most importantly, the intention to walk through this entire journey of decluttering, room by room, habit by habit. You didn't just skim through tips on organizing. You faced the real issues behind clutter, learned to let go without guilt, and discovered how to keep your home feeling like a sanctuary rather than a storage unit.

But let's step back and remember what this was all about. This book wasn't written to help you chase some picture-perfect, minimalist magazine spread. It wasn't about obsessively organizing your socks or owning only 30 items. It was about freedom from stuff that no longer serves you, decisions that drain your energy, and chaos that clouds your peace of mind.

These chapters explored much more than folding techniques and clever storage bins. We addressed the mental fatigue that comes with clutter, how our stuff can silently stress us out, and how our homes often reflect the pace and pressure of our lives. And then, step by step, we flipped the script.

What You've Accomplished (Even If You Don't Feel "Finished")

Let's recap how far you've come:

- You started by understanding why decluttering feels so hard and realized that it's not about laziness or messiness but about emotions, mental overload, and the sheer weight of decision-making.

- Then, you learned a simple, step-by-step system to tackle

clutter in manageable chunks without burnout or drama.

- You tackled the most complex part: knowing where to start. From junk drawers to closets to rooms, you found your way confidently and clearly.

- Each major space in your home, from the bedroom, kitchen, and living room to closets and storage zones, received a fresh, thoughtful look. You didn't just toss things; you evaluated, edited, and made choices based on what serves you now.

- You faced the emotional weight of sentimental items head-on and found healthier ways to honor your past without sacrificing your present.

- You learned how to build sustainable habits, from the "One In, One Out" rule to the 5-minute daily resets so that clutter doesn't sneak back in unintended.

- And maybe most importantly, you figured out how to navigate decluttering in a shared home, how to deal with reluctant partners, overwhelmed kids, and a family that doesn't always jump on board right away.

That's no small feat. And if you ever doubted whether you could do it, this book proves that you are already doing it.

What This Book Promised—and Delivered

I promised this wouldn't be about guilt or extreme minimalism from the beginning. I didn't ask you to part with everything you own or declutter your entire home in one weekend. Instead, I gave you a new lens and way to look at your stuff, space, and life. You now have a system that works, is realistic, and respects your time, energy, and family dynamic.

You were also promised something deeper: a home that supports your well-being. Not just a cleaner kitchen or a tidier bedroom, but a place that feels lighter when you walk into it. A place that reflects your values, pace, and dreams.

You have all the tools now: the checklists, the mindset shifts, the habits, the rules, the starter spaces, and some clever tricks. But above all, you've got the clarity. You know now that decluttering isn't just a task; it's a lifestyle choice that opens the door to more peace, presence, and space for what matters.

Your Next Steps: Keep the Momentum Going

Before we wrap things up completely, let's ground this moment with a few simple, practical next steps so your progress doesn't stall here.

Here's your post-book action plan:

- **The 5-Minute Habit (Daily Reset):** Set a timer for five minutes at the end of each day. Tidy up what's out of place, put away that coffee mug, toss junk mail, and fold the blanket. It's a small task with a big payoff: your home stays in order without you even realizing it.

- **Monthly Declutter Check-In:** Once a month, choose one small area, like your bathroom cabinet or fridge, and do a quick 10–15-minute reset. This keeps clutter from building up and eliminates the need for massive weekend cleanups. Pro tip: set a recurring phone reminder so you never forget.

- **Annual Deep Declutter:** Use seasonal shifts or spring cleaning as a chance to check what no longer fits your space or lifestyle. You don't need to go big; you just need to be focused. The more you maintain throughout the year, the easier this yearly refresh becomes.

- **Pick One Small Habit This Week:** Whether it's doing a nightly 5-minute reset or cleaning off one surface a day, choose one simple thing and commit. Small steps done consistently are the secret to lasting change.

- **Revisit Your Clutter Hot Spots:** Every home has a few sneaky zones where clutter likes to gather. Set a monthly reminder to reset those areas before they become overwhelming again.

- **Use the "One In, One Out" Rule:** Every time you bring something new into your home, whether it's a sweater, a coffee mug, or a new toy, make it a habit to let one item go. This keeps clutter from building back up without needing a full purge.

- **Mark a Quarterly Declutter Refresh Day:** Every three months, choose one day to lightly sweep through drawers, shelves, and storage. You'll be surprised how quickly it goes when you're not starting from scratch.

- **Involve Your Family:** Clutter isn't a one-person problem; it's a household habit. Share what's working, lead by example, and invite everyone to be part of the process. The goal isn't perfection; it's teamwork.

Think of your home as a garden. You don't just weed it once and expect it to stay perfect forever. It needs light tending, occasional pruning, and care throughout the seasons. That's exactly how decluttering works; it's not a one-time project but a gentle rhythm you build into your lifestyle.

I know it's easy to feel like you can't do anything about stuff creeping back in every now and then. But this book should have taught you that you are in charge of the flow. Clutter doesn't just happen to you. You can actively shape your space. You can set boundaries. You can rewrite the story your home tells.

Some days, your house will be messier than others. Life happens. But now, you know what to do about it. You've broken the cycle. You know how to start, how to sustain, and how to reset when needed. You're no longer reacting to clutter; you're responding with intention.

The clutter-free life isn't about everything being perfect all the time. It's about feeling empowered to make choices supporting your peace, pace, and priorities. That's the magic of this whole process, and it's yours now.

THANK YOU

I sincerely thank you for purchasing this book and taking the time to explore its pages. If you enjoyed this book or found it helpful, please consider sharing your experience by leaving an honest review on Amazon.

Your feedback is the best way to support an independent author and publisher.

Thank you for your support!

Printed in Dunstable, United Kingdom